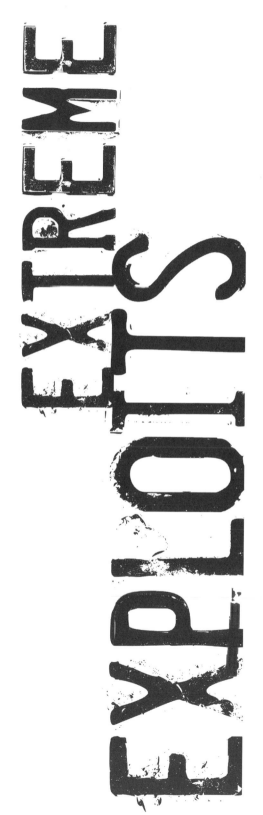

EXTREME EXPLOITS

EXTREME

LIVING
ON THE
EDGE
WITH
JESUS

EXPLOITS

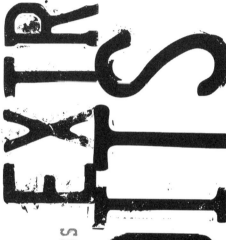

DANNY LOVETT WITH DILLON BURROUGHS

B&H
PUBLISHING GROUP

Nashville, Tennessee

978-0-8054-4861-0

Published by B&H Publishing Group,
Nashville, Tennessee

Dewey Decimal Classification: 248.834
Subject Heading: CHRISTIAN LIFE \
COLLEGE STUDENTS

Unless otherwise noted, Scripture quotations are from
the Holman Christian Standard Bible®, copyright ©
1999, 2000, 2002, 2003 by Holman Bible Publishers.

Other versions include: NKJV, New King James Version,
copyright © 1979, 1980, 1982, Thomas Nelson, Inc.,
Publishers; NIV, New International Version, copyright
© 1973, 1978, 1984, by International Bible Society; NLT,
New Living Translation, copyright © 1996,
used by permission of Tyndale House Publishers, Inc.,
Wheaton, IL 60189 USA. All rights reserved.;
and KJV, King James Version.

1 2 3 4 5 6 7 8 • 13 12 11 10 09

I dedicate this book to my students over the years from Tennessee Temple University and Liberty University.

CONTENTS

Foreword

If anyone can write *Extreme Exploits* with energy, experience, and contagious enthusiasm, it is my friend, Danny Lovett. We are living in times when students long for positive role models. However, those looked to as leaders today often provide unhealthy examples, whether it's a celebrity arrested for misconduct, an athlete competing outside of the rules, or a negative situation with a parent, friend, or loved one. Many students turn to their peers, yet find that even the best of friends occasionally let them down. Where can today's students turn for influences to guide their spiritual growth?

The ideal source is found in the lives of young people who followed God throughout the pages of the Bible. Danny Lovett and Dillon Burroughs's book *Extreme Exploits* does just that. Based on profiles of men and women who followed God despite tremendous opposition from their surrounding culture, this book's message provides insightful guidance for those who seek to influence their own world today.

More than simply another Bible study, however, my friends Danny and Dillon pour passion and application into the words they share. Whether through Esther's decision to stand for her people or Daniel's choice to suffer death rather than give up prayer, the stories spring to life anew to inspire readers.

If I can offer one prayer for you as you read these pages, it would be for you to become a man or woman whose life deeply reflects the biblical role models shared in this book. Only by conforming to God's Word and ultimately becoming more Christlike in the process, will you change your life and influence others for eternity.

I am confident God will use *Extreme Exploits* to encourage and equip many next-generation leaders to become more passionate in their pursuit to follow Christ. As I often say to others, any old bush will do to set on fire with the fire of God. It doesn't matter where you've been but that you align your mind to the mind of God through the Word of God and prepare to be used by the living, redeeming God who created you for His pleasure!

—Kay Arthur

—Dr. Kay Arthur is the co-CEO of Precept Ministries International (PMI) operating in one hundred fifty countries and in seventy languages. She is the best-selling author of more than one hundred books and Bible studies, and host of the international radio and television program *Precepts for Life* along with David Arthur, ThM, who serves as Vice President of Teaching and Training of PMI.

Introduction

FACING THE CHALLENGE

WARNING: *Extreme Exploits* is not for everyone.
It is required reading only for those up to the
challenge of a radical, self-sacrificing, supernatural
commitment to the God of the universe.

I am on a quest for a unique kind of student. You might
be just the kind of person I'm seeking. But I'm not
the only one. God is looking for a few good men and
women too: "For the eyes of the LORD range throughout
the earth to show Himself strong for those *whose hearts
are completely His*" (2 Chronicles 16:9, emphasis added).

Let's be real: aren't you tired of living around cafeteria Christians who think Christianity is a buffet where
they can pick and choose what they want to believe?
I'm searching for those adventurers who want to take
their relationship with Christ seriously and serve God

1

passionately. Joshua said, "But if it doesn't please you to worship the LORD, choose for yourselves today the one you will worship: . . . As for me and my family, we will worship the LORD" (Joshua 24:15).

One of America's buzzwords today when discussing faith is "balance." *Everything* needs to be balanced. Too often that means balancing biblical truth with cultural norms. On Sundays, many people go to church and put on a Christian face, but the rest of their week is no different from anyone else's. Why?

Some call this balance. But this is *not* what Jesus has called us to as followers of Christ. Someone once claimed that Christians have just enough church in the world and just enough world in the church that it is hard to tell them apart. If that's what balance means, let's be *un*balanced. Let's follow the advice of the apostle Paul, who said, "Do not be conformed to this age" (Romans 12:2).

Becoming Difference-Makers

One of the early Christian symbols of the church was a ship on the sea. Throughout the Bible the sea is used as a metaphor for the world. Ships were *made* for the sea, and it's a good thing when ships are in the water. As followers of Christ, we live in this world to make a difference. But when the sea gets into the ship, there is a problem.

That's why it is so important to cultivate a new generation of Christ-followers prepared to live without compromise in a compromising world. Now, more than ever, our culture needs people like you who will *live out* what they believe rather than trying to fit in with the world. As the apostle Paul wrote, "Do not love the world or the things that belong to the world. If anyone loves the world, love for the Father is not in him" (1 John 2:15).

Whenever people have accomplished something significant in any field throughout history, it has taken extreme commitment. In 1912 Ernest Shackleton placed an advertisement for his Imperial Trans-Antarctic Expedition in a British newspaper. Money was short, so the brief ad simply stated his goal. The response was so overwhelming that advertisers today call it the most effective advertisement in the history of print media. The ad read:

> Men wanted for hazardous journey. Small wages, bitter cold, long months of complete darkness, constant danger, safe return doubtful. Honor and recognition in case of success.

If young men in Britain responded *en masse* to that kind of challenge to explore a frozen world of ice at the bottom of the planet, certainly there must be Christian students who are willing to rise to the challenge of following Christ with passion.

Consider the call of Christ to His first followers. When Jesus saw four fishermen and decided to invite them to be His disciples, He said, "Come after Me, and I will make you become fishers of men" (Mark 1:17 NKJV).

How did they respond? *"Immediately* they left their nets and followed Him" (Mark 1:18, emphasis added).

3

I suppose there are a lot of people who would give up the hard work of fishing to follow Jesus, but look at what these guys left behind. "Immediately He called them, and they left their *father* Zebedee in the boat with the *hired men* and followed Him" (Mark 1:20, emphasis added). There are not many people who are eager to follow Jesus when it requires abandoning the comforts of home and a lifestyle that involves serving rather than being served.

Jesus challenged His listeners that:

> If anyone wants to come with Me, he must deny himself, take up his cross daily, and follow Me. For whoever wants to save his life will lose it, but whoever loses his life because of Me will save it. What is a man benefited if he gains the whole world, yet loses or forfeits himself? For whoever is ashamed of Me and My words, the Son of Man will be ashamed of him when He comes in His glory and that of the Father and the holy angels. (Luke 9:23–26)

Jesus was looking for followers who would rise to the challenge of becoming all that God intended them to be. Are you ready to become that kind of person?

In my role as a speaker and president of Tennessee Temple University, I work with thousands of students every year. In the process I meet many youth and college leaders with different ideas about what it takes to reach the next generation. Some think the key is to lower the commitment level to make involvement easier. If

Shackleton had hired them as advertising consultants, his ad might have read something like this:

> Members wanted for adventure trek. Low cost, cool sights, lots of fun nights, ultimate thrills, insurance available. Get your picture in *Extreme Adventure* magazine.

That approach will reach people, but the impact is weak and limited. Fortunately there is a growing movement of next-generation Christian leaders who understand that students today are not really interested in wasting their time or their lives. They want to do something *significant*.

When students understand the high standards of the life to which Christ calls His followers, many are eager to respond. Those youth and college leaders who raise the bar of excellence will be the ones who effectively reach this generation with the truth of Christ. They will become the Shadrachs, Meshachs, Abednegos, and Daniels of our time (Daniel 3).

About three hundred years after Christ's time on earth, a Roman soldier stationed in Egypt finished his tour of duty and was converted to Christianity. He noticed that many spiritual Christians would go into the desert to live alone and meditate on God. Pachomius (pronounced Puh-CHO-mee-us), this new Christian, decided to do this himself, but while he was meditating alone in the desert, he came to believe that an angel told him, "Stay here and build a monastery and many will come to you to be monks."

Pachomius and his brother John built a small building, and soon others came to join them. Initially the community did not have many rules. He decided everyone could keep his own possessions and expected them to contribute as needed to the good of the community. But it was not long until people began complaining about the way Pachomius led the community. In light of these problems, changes were made.

Pachomius later disbanded the community and began a new monastery. This time he established high standards. Those who would join this community would have to give up *everything* to be part of the new movement. Before moving in, the would-be monks were required to memorize twenty chapters from Psalms and two of Paul's New Testament books! This time, Pachomius experienced phenomenal success. Within thirty years, he was operating eleven monasteries and overseeing more than 10,000 men and women who lived in those communities, all by challenging people to a deeper commitment to Christ.

I am not suggesting that you move into a desert monastery, but I am looking for people with that level of commitment. God is seeking students who love Him and want to follow Him 100 percent. He is searching for young men and women willing to live with integrity and without compromise in a culture desperately in need of truth. He is longing for someone *just like you* who will take the message of Christ into the spiritual deserts of this world and make a difference for God.

In this book, I'll share life principles from young people in the Bible who chose to live on the edge with God and how their lives made an eternal impact. During our journey, we'll discover eight essential keys to experiencing the Christian life the way Jesus intended. *Extreme Exploits* will challenge you to live every moment of your life to its fullest potential.

Are you ready? Then let's begin the adventure of living a life passionately devoted to Christ!

Chapter 1

FACING THE GIANTS

Defeat Your Greatest Threats

There are two kinds of Christians today: transformers and conformers. Paul makes it very clear what kind of people God has called us to be: "Do not be conformed to this age, but be transformed by the renewing of your mind, so that you may discern what is the good, pleasing, and perfect will of God" (Romans 12:2).

This is a message we must each seriously consider. Every one of us is either a transformer or conformer. Either we will *transform* our school, our church, our workplace, our city, or our home through a life devoted to Christ, or we will *conform* to the world around us. The book of Daniel tells the story of four Jewish teenagers who chose to be transformers rather than conformers. We'll look at their example later in this book, but first let's consider another emerging follower of Christ who made a difference in his world.

This young man was a transformer, not a conformer, in his generation. He faced incredible obstacles with limited resources, but, in an unlikely circumstance, rose to the challenge and became a national hero. Even years after his death, it was said of him that he "served his own generation by the will of God" (Acts 13:36 NKJV).

Only a Boy Named David

As a teenager David lived during a time when there were not many heroes to look up to in Israel. Saul had been the nation's leader for most of David's life. David remembered the stories his father and uncles told of the past when Saul showed outstanding potential in governing Israel. But those days were gone, and Saul proved himself a dismal failure. The prophet who had anointed Saul as king had announced that God would replace him with another man who was more worthy to be king. At that point David was one of the few in Israel who knew the secret—that he would become the next leader of Israel.

But no one was treating David like a king yet. He would face many barriers before he reached his nation's equivalent of the White House. On the day Samuel arrived at David's home to anoint him as the next king, his own dad, Jesse, had left him in the field to care for the sheep. In the meantime, Jesse paraded David's brothers before the prophet Samuel as potential candidates for the distinguished appointment. Apparently Jesse assumed that David would never make the cut. But this was not surprising. Apart from Samuel, no one else was considering David as king yet either.

Then something happened in the Valley of Elah that catapulted an unknown shepherd boy into the role of national hero. The events of that day would make him a leader in Israel's military and a close personal friend of Israel's crown prince. But he first had to cross a giant-sized barrier. His name was Goliath.

For David, Goliath was a very real, physical giant who stood between him and accomplishing God's purpose for his life. God had called David to be king. As king, he had a responsibility to protect God's people, the nation of Israel.

God has a different purpose for each of our lives, but just like David, you will encounter *very real obstacles* to overcome as you pursue God's purpose. You will face your own personal equivalent of Goliath in your life.

In fact, you may be facing a Goliath right now. Giants and Goliaths come in many shapes and sizes, but one thing is certain: *You are either facing a giant right now, or you will meet one soon.* These giants are huge. They always appear overwhelming. And they are ready to battle against *you*. Is there a giant standing in your way today?

Satan and his dark spiritual forces have an organized army of Goliaths ready to destroy you. That is why the Bible says, "Be strong in the Lord and in his mighty power. Put on all of God's armor so that you will be able to stand firm against all strategies of the devil" (Ephesians 6:10–11 NLT). The Greek word translated *strategies* in these verses means "a method, artifice, cunning, fraud."[1] It describes the way the devil will use Goliaths in his attempt to frustrate and defeat you in your Christian life. Or, as the next verse in that chapter states,

> For we do not wrestle against flesh and blood,
> but against principalities, against powers,
> against the rulers of the darkness of this age,
> against spiritual hosts of wickedness in the
> heavenly places. (Ephesians 6:12 NKJV)

Your Goliaths have ruthless purposes to *destroy* you, to *defeat* you, and to *decommission* you. How do Goliaths come? They come strategically and very powerfully. The Greek word translated *principalities* in Ephesians 6:12 means "beginning, principality," and is also translated as *power*.[2] Satan always has a champion, a cosmic force that seeks to exploit your most vulnerable weaknesses.

Your Goliath could be a sexual temptation, such as online pornography. Your Goliath could be an addiction like alcohol or drugs. It could be money, music, a divorce in your family, popularity, video games, your GPA, your pride, sports, or even your friends. It could be an unhealthy relationship with a boyfriend or girlfriend. Satan wants to use your Goliath to destroy you.

One of my Goliaths was a bad home situation. I was kicked out of my home when I was eleven years old. In extreme situations, your Goliath could even be the death of a loved one. That was my greatest Goliath.

The Night Goliath Came to Tuscaloosa

In 1980, after attending Liberty Baptist Theological Seminary, I moved my young family to Tuscaloosa, Alabama. I believed God had called us to build a great church for His glory and the good of the community. I had only been in town two weeks when Goliath arrived uninvited to our home.

I had finished my graduate coursework in December and accepted the invitation of thirty-five people in Tuscaloosa, Alabama, to help them reach their community for Christ. On New Year's Eve we had 135 people come together for a special gathering. I had invited one of my professors to speak that night and stay for the weekend. That evening I also challenged those at our gathering to commit to the task of starting a life-changing church.

At the end we offered a time for people to make spiritual decisions. I wanted to lead by example and knelt with my wife and eight-year-old son. We were the first ones to tell God we were willing to do whatever was necessary and give whatever was needed in order to see our church make a difference for Christ. We really meant what we said when we prayed that night, but we had no idea how challenging the days ahead would be, or that God would test our commitment through tragedy.

That night my wife and I were up until 4:00 a.m. talking with my professor and his wife. We spent hours discussing our hopes and dreams for the future. When we finally did go to bed, I turned to my wife and said, "I love you." I remember her saying she loved me and believed God would use us to make a difference for Him in Tuscaloosa. I will never forget that night.

My spiritual Goliath arrived at about 6:15 a.m. We had only been asleep a couple of hours when my wife woke me up. It was obvious she was in trouble. She was having an acute asthma attack and couldn't breathe.

Prior to serving as a pastor, I had been a paramedic, so I knew my wife's attack was very serious. I helped her to the couch and called 911. Soon everyone in the house was awake. My professor's wife took my son to another room while my professor and I tried to assist my wife as we waited for the ambulance. But before the ambulance arrived, her eyes rolled back into her head and she fell into cardiac arrest. Her lungs had filled with fluid. She was suffocating.

The next ten minutes were the longest minutes of my life. I tried everything I could to save her. When the paramedics arrived, they took over the CPR. They quickly left the house with my wife, my professor drove my car, and we followed the ambulance to the hospital emergency room. Within a half hour several people from our church had learned of my wife's condition and arrived at the hospital to be with us. But thirty-five minutes after we arrived, the doctor came into the waiting room looking for me. I can still hear his voice today:

"I'm sorry to tell you this, but your wife did not make it. She's dead."

I could not believe what I heard. All I could say was, "No, it's not possible!" She was only twenty-eight years old. I had just finished my education. We had just moved to start a new church. This could *not* be happening. Not *now*!

But the doctor's report was true. Firmly, but gently, he repeated the news I dreaded to hear. *"I'm sorry. She is dead."*

The Devil's Giant-Sized Goals

There is no doubt in my mind that spiritual forces of evil wanted to stop me in my tracks that night before I even started. Jesus said, "A thief comes only to steal and to kill and to destroy. I have come that they may have life and have it in abundance" (John 10:10).

When Goliath challenged Israel with his shouts across the Valley of Elah, one of his goals was to embarrass God's people and ridicule their God. Goliaths always try to bring *shame* into your life. That is why Satan wants you to cross the line with your boyfriend or girlfriend. That is why you might sometimes be tempted to run away from home. That is why Satan wants you to disrespect your mom or dad. His goal is to bring shame on you, your family, and your integrity. That is also why he wants pastors and church leaders to struggle or fall into immorality so he can bring shame on the church.

When Saul and his army heard the words of the giant Philistine, they were discouraged and fearful. That was one of Goliath's goals. Satan constantly desires to *discourage* you. If he succeeds, he will stop your progress in following Christ. The Hebrew word translated *dismayed* in 1 Samuel 17:11 means "to become broken, cast down."[3] Satan wants to leave you powerless in your walk with God and relationships with other people. Fear is his best tool to accomplish that goal.

Your Goliaths also want to *dismiss* you. "When the Philistine looked and saw David, he despised him because he was just a youth, healthy and handsome. He said to David, 'Am I a dog that you come against me with sticks?' Then he cursed David by his gods" (1 Samuel 17:42–43).

Goliath belittled David. He cursed David. He laughed at David. Goliath looked down on him and said, "Hey, little guy. You think you can take me on? You're nothing. I'm going to kill you! By the time I'm finished with you, I'll feed you to the birds."

The giants the devil sends your way want to *destroy* you. "'Come here,' the Philistine called to David, 'and I'll give your flesh to the birds of the sky and the wild beasts!'" (17:44). Goliath continued his tirade against David just as giants will in your life. "Bring it on! It's a good day to die, and I'm here to help you out. I'll rip your body into pieces and leave you for the animals to clean up."

Given the circumstances, if I were David, I think I would have been scared to death. But David didn't fear Goliath, and we do not need to be afraid of the giants we face in life. "For God has not given us a spirit of fearfulness, but one of power, love, and sound judgment" (2 Timothy 1:7). We are on the winning side. Nothing but victory is possible. As Paul wrote, "If God is for us, who is against us? He did not even spare His own Son, but offered Him up for us all; how will He not also with Him grant us everything?" (Romans 8:31–32).

A word of caution: the thief is still out there seeking to kill, steal, and destroy. That is why the apostle Peter told Christians facing their own Goliaths to

Be sober! Be on the alert! Your adversary the Devil is prowling around like a roaring lion, looking for anyone he can devour. Resist him, firm in the faith, knowing that the same sufferings are being experienced by your brothers in the world. (1 Peter 5:8 9)

It might not feel like it at the time, but *your* Goliath is really not that different from those faced by other Christians around the world every day. If you tap into the resources God has made available to you, you are guaranteed victory over your Goliath. You can count on it. It is the promise of God. Your victory has more to do with *who God is* than *what you can do*. We don't need to go to God and say, "Here is my problem." We need to go to our problem and say, "Here is my God."

The apostle Paul said it another way:

No temptation has overtaken you except what is common to humanity. God is faithful and He will not allow you to be tempted beyond what you are able, but with the temptation He will also provide a way of escape, so that you are able to bear it. (1 Corinthians 10:13)

Young People Who Ruled the World

David was not the first young man to face giant-sized problems in life. One of the greatest, yet nearly forgotten heroes of the Old Testament was a young guy named Joseph. Joseph's entire life was a series of encounters with giants. As each giant crossed his path, he understood God had a purpose in his life, and he moved beyond that giant to face the next challenge God had in store for him.

To start, Joseph was born into a severely dysfunctional family. His father had children with four different women, leaving Joseph with eleven brothers plus a few additional sisters. Joseph also happened to be the son of his dad's favorite wife, which gained him some privileges along the way, but also earned him the jealousy of his brothers.

Early in his life, Joseph had dreams in which he believed God was assuring him that he would someday become a man of great influence. He claimed the day would come when even the members of his own family would bow down before him. As you could imagine, that kind of talk did not help relieve the family tensions that already existed. His brothers began to sarcastically call him "the Dreamer" (see Genesis 37:19).

His father viewed Joseph as his favorite son and displayed that affection in front of other family members. When he gave Joseph a "coat of many colors," his brothers certainly understood the message that was implied. In the agricultural culture of that day, men wore short tunics when working in the field. The managers wore longer, more colorful coats as a symbol of their authority over others. Every time Joseph put on his jacket, the resentment grew in the hearts of his brothers. It was only natural that hostility would eventually erupt into hateful rage.

The day came when Joseph's brothers had their chance. In a farm field far from their father's home, the brothers captured Joseph, ripped off his jacket, and threw him into a pit intending to kill him. They ignored Joseph's desperate pleas for his life. When a caravan of traveling traders passed by, they took advantage of the opportunity and sold their brother as a slave.

In Egypt, Joseph served faithfully in his new master's home and quickly rose to leadership. It was not long before his master's wife saw the attractive new slave and began making plans of her own. She invited him into a sexual relationship, despite the fact that she was already married. Joseph turned her down and refused to compromise his convictions. "How could I do such a great evil and sin against God?" he asked (Genesis 39:9).

But that did not stop Potiphar's wife. "Although she spoke to Joseph day after day, he refused to go to bed with her" (39:10). Every day, as Joseph worked for his master, he faced his Goliath, and this time Goliath wore perfume! Yet each day he refused to compromise his convictions and give in to her temptations. When she realized she would not get her way with him, she falsely accused him of attempted rape and had him sent to prison.

Even in the face of this new Goliath, an Egyptian jail, Joseph remained faithful to God. His faithfulness to God in the darkest hours of his life became apparent to those around him. Even when those he helped in prison forgot him for two years, he did not turn bitter despite thirteen years in prison. Instead, he allowed God to use these giant-sized problems to make him better. And God was faithful. Having overcome a series of Goliaths in his life, Joseph was promoted to one of Egypt's highest political offices at only thirty years old.

Joseph understood that God uses problems in our lives to accomplish His purposes, even when those who cause the problems have a different intent. Years later Joseph explained this concept to his brothers when they wondered why he was not bitter: "You planned evil against me; God planned it for good to bring about the present result—the survival of many people" (Genesis 50:20).

Each time you stand before a Goliath in your life, remember that the giant somehow fits into the larger purpose God has for your life. God intends good for your life today: "We know that all things work together for the good of those who love God: those who are called according to His purpose" (Romans 8:28).

It was not just young men who have accomplished great things for God. One of the most influential people during the Jewish captivity was a young Jewish girl named Hadassah. Most people know her better by her Persian name Esther.

Esther became queen of Persia as a result of winning a beauty pageant held after the previous queen had embarrassed her husband. While living in the palace, Esther learned that one of her husband's closest advisors had masterminded the extinction of her race. She was confident that she could escape the genocide because no one knew she was Jewish, but her uncle who had raised her challenged her to take on this giant. "Who knows, perhaps you have come to the kingdom for such a time as this," he said (Esther 4:14).

Like David, Esther knew this was a worthy cause. This giant had to be defeated. She realized that she could not stand back and watch these murders take place, but she was not sure she would survive in the process. She came to the conclusion that she had to take on this giant and save her people, even if it cost her life. She asked her people to go without food or water for three nights in preparation for her intervention with the king. Esther determined, "I will go to the king even if it is against the law. If I perish, I perish" (4:16). But Esther did not die. God used her to preserve the Jewish people. Still today, her heroism is celebrated by Jews around the world each year during the Feast of Purim.

Discovering the Real You

Every giant you face will reveal your true self. You may not face many major problems in your life, but when you do it will become apparent what kind of person you are. You can pick a red apple from the tree, but you really do not know how it tastes until you bite into it. Likewise, you will not know how strong you are in your faith until something bites into you.

When Saul and his army met Goliath, they panicked. They were scared. To put it bluntly, they were cowards. According to the Bible, "When all the Israelite men saw Goliath, they retreated from him terrified" (1 Samuel 17:24). When they started toward the battle, everybody thought they were brave warriors. Yet they soon discovered that they were not brave at all. None of them would take a stand for God. Nobody knew they were cowards until they had to face Goliath. But when David met the same giant, he stood for what was right. When it was over, he became a national hero.

Those who rise to giant positions in life have defeated the giants they have met along the way. That is what David did. Passionate followers of Christ will grow to have significant influence, yet problems are an essential tool God uses in our lives throughout the growth process. Don't forget that our problems and disappointments are God's divine appointments.

The disciple closest to Jesus, named Peter, wrote, "Dear friends, when the fiery ordeal arises among you to test you, don't be surprised by it, as if something unusual were happening to you. Instead, as you share in the sufferings of the Messiah rejoice, so that you may also rejoice with great joy at the revelation of His glory" (1 Peter 4:12–13). James, the brother of Jesus, also shared, "Consider it a great joy, my brothers, whenever you experience various trials, knowing that the testing of your faith produces endurance" (James 1:2–3).

There is plenty of room at the top for radical, fully devoted followers of Christ. God is an "I can" God, not an "I can't" God. David could have said, "I can't." The whole army said, "I can't." But David said, "I can."

"I am able to do all things *through* Him who strengthens me" (Philippians 4:13, emphasis added). That is the key. There will be many times you will face challenges that you cannot handle on your own. Jesus said, "You can do nothing without Me" (John 15:5). But God does not expect us to face our giants on our own. Remember, "Nothing will be impossible with God" (Luke 1:37).

Many successful ministry and business leaders have one thing in common—they have faced major personal tragedies in their lives and have overcome them. Perhaps that is why God uses the word *overcome* thirteen times in the New Testament to describe Christians.[4] "For whatever is born of God overcomes the world. And this is the victory that has *overcome* the world—our faith" (1 John 5:4 NKJV, emphasis added). Giants are often tools God uses to shape us for bigger things.

The Israelites could not enter the Promised Land until they passed through the land of giants. Their victory over their enemies was delayed *forty years* because they failed to have faith in God to overcome the giants in their path.

God had promised them the land, but ten of the twelve spies discouraged them: "We even saw the Nephilim there." (The offspring of Anak were descended from the Nephilim.) "To ourselves we seemed like grasshoppers, and we must have seemed the same to them" (Numbers 13:33). Only Joshua and Caleb survived that generation, and they lived to see the giants fall.

At the age of eighty-five, Caleb still believed that God was bigger than the biggest giant. He asked his old friend Joshua for permission to build his retirement home on the same mountain where they had spotted those giants forty-five years earlier. "Now give me this hill country the LORD promised [me] on that day, because you heard then that the Anakim are there, as well as large fortified cities. Perhaps the LORD will be with me and I will drive them out as the LORD promised" (Joshua 14:12).

Years later David faced his giant and was catapulted into a position of prominent leadership in Israel. Ironically, that giant was a direct descendant of the same giants who had terrorized Israel generations earlier and turned Caleb into an overcomer.

Even though that line of giants came to an end under David's leadership, others confronted people throughout God's Word. For Daniel, it was a night in a room full of hungry lions. Daniel trusted God, and the lions lost their appetite for the night. For Shadrach, Meshach, and Abednego, it was a visit to Nebuchadnezzar's flaming furnace. The trio trusted God, and the furnace turned into little more than a tanning salon.

Somewhere out there, a giant is waiting for you. You can let it terrorize you into weakening your commitment to Christ, or you can trust God and claim His promise: "You are from God, little children, and you have conquered them, because the One who is in you is greater than the one who is in the world" (1 John 4:4).

The choice is yours to make. Who are you going to believe? As you make that choice, remember that you will never experience everything God has for you until you get ready to face your giant and win.

⊡ THINK ABOUT IT ⊡

1. This chapter begins with the claim that there are two kinds of Christians: transformers and conformers. Which group best describes you? Why? Which group would you *like* to belong to? Do you think God could use you as a transformer in your world? What would it take to get there?

2. David would have to cross many barriers before he officially became king. What kinds of barriers will you have to cross to pursue God's vision for your life? Which ones do you think you can handle on your own? Which ones will you need help with? What is the biggest Goliath in your way right now?

3. Remember the story about "The Night Goliath Came to Tuscaloosa, Alabama"? Why does the devil do what he does in our lives? How can God help you break free from the devil's hold on your life in these areas? What is the first thing you need to do to experience victory over the devil instead of defeat?

4. This chapter tells the story of several young individuals who were used by God to change their world. Which of these individuals can you identify with best? From a purely human perspective, why should that person have failed? How did he or she achieve success? What would it take for you to be successful in the same way?

5. God uses the word *overcomer* several times in the New Testament to describe followers of Christ. Read 1 John 5:4 again from this chapter or from your own Bible. How would you describe an overcomer? What does it take to become one?

Chapter 2

WHO'S IN CHARGE?

Decide Who Has Your Allegiance

Sometimes you don't really understand the importance of a decision until years later. What you consider a small decision today could impact the rest of your life, the lives of those around you, and even the lives of future generations. Think it doesn't matter? Think again. Every act of your life influences every future act of your life—and the lives of many others.

God's Godliest Men: Exhibit One—Noah

One of the godliest men of the Bible was Noah. When God called the prophet Ezekiel to announce judgment on Jerusalem for its persistent sin toward God, he said, "'Even if these three men—*Noah*, Daniel, and Job—were in it, they would deliver only themselves by their righteousness.' This is the declaration of the Lord GOD" (Ezekiel 14:14, emphasis added).

Just in case people missed it the first time, God repeated Himself so everyone could catch what He was saying: "'Even if Noah, Daniel, and Job were in it, as I live'—the declaration of the Lord GOD—'they could not deliver their son or daughter. They would deliver only themselves by their righteousness'" (14:20).

When God looked for spiritual examples, these three stood out above all others. They were not the only people of integrity, but were people whose lives stood out in such a way that no one could dispute their character. Under God's law, an individual could not be condemned except by two or three witnesses. Noah, Job, and Daniel were God's three witnesses to condemn an irreverent culture.

Chronologically Noah was the first example God used as a witness against His people. Noah lived in an evil generation. "The LORD saw that the wickedness of man was great in the earth, and that every intent of the thoughts of his heart was only evil continually" (Genesis 6:5 NKJV). It is hard to imagine any stronger language God could have used to describe the lifestyles of the people during that time.

We are told that, "the LORD regretted that He had made man on the earth, and He was grieved in His heart" (6:6). The consequence God selected as a result of their practices was: "I will wipe off the face of the earth: man, whom I created, together with the animals, creatures that crawl, and birds of the sky—for I regret that I made them" (6:7).

Yet in the midst of the hopelessness of that age, there was one person who rose above its evil to live a godly life: "Noah, however, found favor in the eyes of the LORD" (6:8).

How did Noah find favor with God? By faith. That faith not only rescued him from the judgment of God, but also provided an escape for his family and every generation since the flood. As the Bible later mentioned,

> By faith Noah, after being warned about what was not yet seen, in reverence built an ark to deliver his family. By this he condemned the world and became an heir of the righteousness that comes by faith. (Hebrews 11:7)

A single decision impacted the world for generations to come! Noah chose to live differently. He followed God despite the decisions made by the people around him. And the world was never the same.

God's Godliest Men: Exhibit Two—Job

Although Job lived after Noah, many Bible teachers believe Job may have been the first book of the Bible written. The story of Job was well known by God's people who lived in Babylon. He was a man known for his complete allegiance to God, a fact even the devil could not dispute.

The story of Job begins by describing Job as "a man of perfect integrity, who feared God and turned away from evil" (Job 1:1). He would even offer sacrifices in prayer to God just in case someone in his family had committed a wrong. God blessed Job with a large family and wealth. In addition to being a person of integrity, his financial portfolio made him "the greatest man among all the people of the east" (1:3).

Even the devil could not find anything wrong with Job's life. The devil appeared before God and was asked, "Have you considered My servant Job? No one else on earth is like him, a man of perfect integrity, who fears God and turns away from evil" (1:8).

The devil could not dispute God's evaluation of Job's life. Sometimes I wonder if God could brag about me like that. If God mentioned you to Satan, how would Satan respond? For most of us, He would have plenty of bad habits to mention. However, in Job's case, the best the devil could do was make excuses. He accused Job of only serving God because God had blessed him. "But stretch out Your hand and strike everything he owns, and he will surely curse You to Your face," (1:11) he claimed.

God gave Satan permission to take away all He had given to Job. The only restriction was that Job's physical health could not be touched. Satan immediately destroyed Job's wealth and his family with the exception of Job's wife. Yet on the worst day of his life, Job responded, "The LORD gives, and the LORD takes away. Praise the name of the LORD" (1:21).

Job proved Satan wrong and God right. "Throughout all this Job did not sin or blame God for anything" (1:22). At Satan's next meeting with God, Satan asked for permission to harm Job physically to test his true allegiance (see 2:4).

God said yes and Satan hit Job with painful boils over his entire body. Some believe Job had a dreaded disease called elephantitis, a painful condition that causes severe swelling resulting in open sores that continually run the risk of infection. Life was so bad that Job's own wife believed he would be better off if he just cursed God and died. Yet Job continued to live a life of integrity even when his wealth and health disappeared.

God's Godliest Men: Exhibit Three—Daniel

The third example of a godly man referred to by Ezekiel was different. Noah and Job had lived hundreds of years before Ezekiel. Their stories had been told for generations. But Daniel was alive during the time of Ezekiel. Daniel had been taken to Babylon from his Jewish homeland as a slave during the first captivity. Ezekiel had been taken captive a few years later in the second captivity.

Although Daniel had been taken first, he was probably younger than Ezekiel by a decade. When Ezekiel held up Daniel as one of his three men of greatest integrity, Daniel was still a young man. How could Daniel be included with Noah and Job?

Let me shatter one of the great myths about spiritual maturity: *It has nothing to do with your age.* It is simply untrue to believe that older Christians are automatically more mature Christians. Some Christians are physically older but still spiritual infants.

Living without compromise is a choice. It's a choice made by emerging men and women to honor God when faced with opportunities to compromise. It has nothing to do with age. It is about the choices we make and the core values of our lives that govern those choices.

When I travel, I often encounter students who tell me about their struggles to live a life without compromise. As I listen, I know they face unique challenges. Sometimes I wonder how I would have responded if I had faced the same situation.

Yet there is a principle in Job that applies to every difficult moment we face: God never lets something come into our lives until He is convinced we can handle it. If we couldn't, God would not have allowed it in the first place. The apostle Paul wrote,

> No temptation has overtaken you except what
> is common to humanity. God is faithful and He
> will not allow you to be tempted beyond what
> you are able, but with the temptation He will
> also provide a way of escape, so that you are
> able to bear it. (1 Corinthians 10:13)

As a student living in today's world, you may think you have a tough life. You do. But that does not mean you have an impossible life. The people who have been used greatly by Christ have been those who have stood for what is right during the worst of times.

Daniel is a perfect example. When he was a teenager, foreign soldiers invaded his hometown and took him as a hostage into a different country along with several of his friends. There was also a spiritual battle among his culture. He observed Satan attack the lives of other captives, eroding their sense of purpose and meaning in life.

Many of Daniel's young friends compromised and began to follow the practices of the people around them. The only reason Daniel was mentioned among three heroes of the faith was because God called him to stand strong and Daniel chose to obey.

Finding a Purpose Worth Living For

Daniel's choice was not easy. He was not only in a new culture, but he was also selected for specialized training for his new political leader. Ashpenaz, one of Nebuchadnezzar's trusted servants, had been charged to find "young men without any physical defect, good-looking, suitable for instruction in all wisdom, knowledgeable, perceptive, and capable of serving in the king's palace—and to teach them the Chaldean language and literature" (Daniel 1:4).

Daniel, however, knew that God had a different purpose for his life. "Daniel purposed in his heart that he would not defile himself" (1:8 NKJV). The Hebrew word translated *defile* literally means "pollute." Daniel determined to remain pure regardless of what he faced. He could not change his circumstances, but he decided he would not allow those circumstances to shape his character.

The apostle Paul challenged Christians to make a similar commitment to God. He told the Christ-followers in Rome, "Therefore, brothers, by the mercies of God, I urge you to present your bodies as a living sacrifice, holy and pleasing to God; this is your spiritual worship" (Romans 12:1). Paul encouraged his readers to settle the authority issue in their lives once and for all. That is what Daniel did when he "purposed in his heart" (Daniel 1:8 KJV).

To make a decision is not enough. Once you make a decision, you must take the next step and apply your decision. During the summer I like to take my motorcycle out on the open road. When I got my motorcycle license years ago, it was the result of a decision I made to go through the motorcycle training school. I had to learn the rules and laws for riding a motorcycle. The state gave me a test to make sure I knew the rules and had the ability to drive my bike safely. When I ride on a warm summer afternoon, I don't have to decide what to do when I come to a red signal light. That decision was made years ago. All I have to do is implement the decision I have already made.

Once you have made your stand, you don't have to decide what to do every time you face a new challenge. You simply have to follow through with the decision you have already made. The question to ask is not, "What should I do now?" but rather, "How do I apply my decision to stand for what is right?" Your previous decision determines how you answer the challenges of everyday life.

Does that sound like a strange way to live the Christian life? It really shouldn't. It was the way God intended the Christian life. He knew we could not succeed by our own strength. None of us can. So He gave us the only One who could—His Son Jesus. Paul understood this when he wrote, "I no longer live, but Christ lives in me. The life I now live in the flesh, I live by faith in the Son of God, who loved me and gave Himself for me" (Galatians 2:20). That is the key: Not I *but Christ*. When He is in charge, He enables us to live without compromise by living His life through us.

When we let Christ live His life through us, our lives become a living reflection of God's perfect power.

Babylonian Brainwashing

It should not surprise us that Satan is not interested in helping us live for God. Satan is eager to do everything he can to entice us into little compromises until we have abandoned everything we believe. In Daniel's case, he did not have to wait long to see the devil begin trying to undermine his faith in God.

Daniel and his three friends Hananiah, Mishael, and Azariah had been raised by parents who wanted their children to remember God throughout their lives. How do we know? Each of these young men had the suffix *el* or *yah* added to his name. The word *El* was a Hebrew name for God. It was used to describe God's power, like in the creation of the universe.

The word *Yah* was another Hebrew name for God. *Yah* was often used to describe God's *covenant*, His caring relationship with people. Every day of their lives, Daniel, Hananiah, Mishael, and Azariah could not escape the constant reminder of who God was. His name was included in their very names.

One of the first things the Babylonian officials did as part of their educational program was to change the names of the people they took into captivity. Daniel's name was changed to Belteshazzar. Hananaiah became Shadrach, Mishael became Meshach, and Azariah became Abednego. These new names were designed to mark a new beginning, but there was something sinister about the way it was done. Their old Hebrew names that included God's name were removed. Their new names were associated with the names and practices of the Babylonian gods. While there was nothing these young men could do about the actions of the Babylonians, they chose to remember who they were and who they served.

These new names also marked the beginning of a three-year training program, an effort at Babylonian brainwashing designed to make these young Jewish men think, act, and fit into their surrounding culture. Most of us have a much better situation than Daniel and his friends, but we still fail consistently to live without compromise. We can control what we allow to influence us to some degree, but we often make wrong choices and allow the world to influence our thinking.

The apostle Paul wrote, "We demolish arguments and every pretension that sets itself up against the knowledge of God, and *we take captive every thought to make it obedient to Christ*" (2 Corinthians 10:5 NIV, emphasis added). In Daniel's case, his captors thought they could be in control of his thoughts, but they could not remove his faith in God. Daniel had settled the authority issue in his life. Because he was a follower of God, no other power could remove his true allegiance.

What's for Breakfast?

Finally the time came when Daniel and his friends could make decisions about some of the influences in their lives. I like to think of Daniel and his three friends settling in to their new accommodations in Babylon and looking over the breakfast menu before they went to bed that night. There it was, in clear black print. The day would begin with the finest ham in Babylon served with toast and scrambled eggs, along with a glass of freshly squeezed orange juice. For most of us, that would be a great breakfast. But for Daniel, Hananiah, Mishael, and Azariah, this breakfast presented a problem.

One of the ways young Jewish men expressed their faith in God in the Old Testament was by observing the dietary practices given in the Law of Moses. Some experts believe God gave these laws to Israel to keep them healthy and prevent the spread of disease (see Exodus 15:26). Regardless, these food laws were one of the ways God's people demonstrated their faith in a way that stood out from surrounding cultures. It was a daily reminder that God was important in every decision in life. That applied even in a decision as simple as choosing oatmeal over ham and eggs for breakfast.

As these young men considered the situation, they chose not to compromise. They gave up the finest foods the Babylonian palace kitchens could prepare for a simpler, God-honoring diet of grains and vegetables. It doesn't seem like a big deal to us today, but this one decision began a major controversy with their boss.

Ashpenaz was accountable to the king to ensure that those in his care successfully passed through their prescribed training. In three years he had to turn these young Jewish boys into men who fit into the royal court. When Daniel made his request, Ashpenaz responded,

> My lord the king assigned your food and drink.
> I'm afraid of what would happen if he saw your
> faces looking thinner than those of the other
> young men your age. You would endanger my
> life with the king. (Daniel 1:10)

In other words, Ashpenaz could have died if their request didn't work out.

From a personal perspective, Ashpenaz's concerns were reasonable. Unfortunately that still left Daniel and his friends with a problem. To eat the king's selected foods meant they would compromise their faith. They decided to honor God and endure the consequences of their decision. Daniel proposed an idea he hoped would be acceptable to his leader and allow Daniel to honor God.

> Please test your servants for 10 days. Let us be
> given vegetables to eat and water to drink. Then
> examine our appearance and the appearance of
> the young men who are eating the king's food,
> and deal with your servants based on what you
> see. (Daniel 1:12–13)

In the context of three years, ten days does not seem like a long time. But for ten days four young people took a stand to live without compromise. It was not easy. Three times a day they came into the dining hall for a meal of boiled potatoes, grilled carrots, or stir-fried celery. But as they walked down the hall to the banquet room, they could smell crisp bacon being served for breakfast, perhaps smoked ham for lunch, and fresh pork roasted over an open flame for dinner. For ten days they washed down their simple meal with a glass of water while their companions enjoyed the best of the king's wine. Ten days. Thirty consecutive meals. Day after day they remained true to their commitment to live without compromise in Babylon.

That is what it meant when they chose to forfeit the daily provisions of Babylon to remain true to God. Consider the applications for your life. Every day Satan will offer you your equivalent of the best Babylon has to offer. Yet God's Word directs us to

> . . . not love the world or the things that belong
> to the world. If anyone loves the world, love for
> the Father is not in him. Because everything
> that belongs to the world—the lust of the flesh,
> the lust of the eyes, and the pride in one's
> lifestyle—is not from the Father, but is from
> the world. And the world with its lust is passing
> away, but the one who does God's will remains
> forever. (1 John 2:15–17)

You can count on it. Satan's forces will stop by sometime today to tempt you. The offer will look good. But don't be fooled. If it is not of the Father, it won't last. It may be fun for a moment, but that moment will quickly fade. The temporary pleasures of this world fail to measure up to their promises.

The reality is that in Daniel's situation, there should have been an entire banquet hall of young men eating nothing but vegetables. They had all been raised with the same spiritual teaching. They knew what God required when it came to their diet, but they compromised.

There's an old bumper sticker that reads, "What is popular is not always right and what is right is not always popular." This was certainly true for Daniel and his three friends. When tough choices arise, many will choose not to stand for God. But if you have settled the authority issue in your life once and for all, the choice is already made.

As tough as it may be at times to say no to temptation and yes to God, you need to put that decision into action day-by-day. Out of an entire school of people raised to follow God, only four made a decision that their commitment to God was too important for even a small compromise.

In the end God honored their choice. "At the end of 10 days they looked better and healthier than all the young men who were eating the king's food" (Daniel 1:15). When Ashpenaz saw the results for himself, he had no problem extending the trial period. "So the guard continued to remove their food and the wine they were to drink and gave them vegetables" (1:16).

Those who follow God cannot live lives of shame. Those who live a life of compromise are always looking over their shoulders to see if they will get caught. Those who choose to live godly lives boldly stand for God. That is why Paul wrote that in Christ "we have boldness, access, and confidence through faith in Him" (Ephesians 3:12).

The Long-Term Consequences of Eating Right

Most doctors encourage their patients to watch what they eat. They believe if we consistently eat the right foods, we can prevent certain lifestyle diseases from developing. Daniel and his friends made a decision to eat right as an expression of their purpose to honor God in all they did. They didn't realize what would occur as the result of that simple decision. That is often true in our lives. The little decisions we make often impact our lives and the lives of others years later. That's one reason it's important to settle the authority issue once and for all, to be sure every decision you make in life is consistent with your purpose to honor God.

Following this episode with Daniel and his friends, we are told, "God gave these four young men knowledge and understanding in every kind of literature and wisdom. Daniel also understood visions and dreams of every kind" (Daniel 1:17). They stood for God while in a difficult situation. God stood with them by providing the wisdom necessary to stand out among those around them.

But that's not the end of the story. Three years later they appeared before Nebuchadnezzar for examination. They excelled above all others in their class in every way and were quickly employed in the palace. "In every matter of wisdom and understanding that the king consulted them about, he found them 10 times better than all the diviner-priests and mediums in his entire kingdom" (1:20).

Too many students compromise who they are to fit in better with others. Yet every compromise erodes their influence in the world. Daniel cut the word *compromise* out of his dictionary. He simply decided it was not an option. Because he chose to live without compromise, God gave him influence beyond nearly every person of his time. He became a close advisor to King Nebuchadnezzar, the greatest world leader of the time. He survived at least four transitions of power in an age when new rulers routinely executed the advisors of former kings and replaced them with their own friends.

Today historians look back on individuals like Nebuchadnezzar, Darius the Mede, and Cyrus the Persian as great men who changed the course of history. But at some point in their lives, each of these men refused to make a decision without consulting Daniel. They understood the importance of wise counsel and sought the wisest man they knew, a man who was wise enough to realize there were some things in life that could not be compromised.

And to think, it all began with a simple decision of what to eat for breakfast.

⊠ THINK ABOUT IT ⊠

1. The Bible compares the days of Noah to the time just before Christ will return to earth. How is our world similar to the world of Noah before the Flood? What would it take for you to stand out as a committed follower of Christ?

2. Review Job 1:13–19; 2:7. List the problems Job faced. Have you found yourself facing some of these same problems? What other problems could you add to that list in your own life? How can you trust God to help you in your current situation?

3. Daniel was one of Ezekiel's Top Three because he was true to God's purpose in his life. What are God's purposes for your life? Are you prepared to be true to them with the same intensity as Daniel?

4. Daniel and those exiled in Babylon with him faced several subtle and overt efforts to change their core values. What are some of the temptations we face to compromise? What is one cultural value you need to work on changing this week, or one of God's values that needs reinforcing?

5. Every action produces a consequence—sometimes good, sometimes bad. What were the consequences of Daniel's obedience to God? As you look over the things you did in the past week, what are the likely consequences of those actions? What needs to change in the way you live this week?

Chapter 3

A WINNING ATTITUDE

Discover What It Takes to Be a Champion

Do you sometimes wonder if you will ever be able to overcome some of the overwhelming obstacles in your life that seem too hard to handle? There are two unlikely overcomers in the Bible whose stories should give us hope that we can defeat our giants—King David and Moses, the leader of God's people from Egypt.

David: An Unlikely Hero

David discovered that the only way to make his giant go away was to defeat him. Goliath would not leave. David could not pretend he was an illusion or did not exist. And the longer God's people waited, the worse the ridicule grew.

Goliath appeared for forty straight days in the Valley of Elah to mock God's people and call for a warrior brave enough to confront him. Many naturally expected King Saul to step up to the challenge. He was king and the tallest guy on their team. But Saul was intimidated. For forty days he hid and lived in indecision.

God's people, the army of Israel, hid in the trenches. They stayed just close enough to listen to Goliath's taunts, but far enough away to escape personal harm. They thought they would be safe if they could just stay out of his reach.

It was not until David arrived that Goliath was confronted. But why David? He wasn't even a soldier in the army. Why did this young shepherd stand up to Goliath when his king and entire army would not? The answers to these questions can help us rise to the challenge and live without compromise in the face of our own spiritual battles.

You Don't Become a Hero Overnight

Heroes aren't born heroes. David didn't begin life as a mighty warrior. He did not begin life as a great soldier. David's first introduction to King Saul was as the king's musician (see 1 Samuel 16:18). Saul asked David to play music for him when he was depressed. When Saul met him, he liked David so much he selected him as his armor-bearer (see 16:21). It wasn't until later that David became a national celebrity, which led to David's promotion to commander in Saul's army (see 18:5).

David began small. In reality, small is often God's training ground for big. For instance, in the parable of the talents told by Jesus, those who were faithful in small things were commended. They were told, "Well done, good and faithful slave! You were faithful over a few things; I will put you in charge of many things. Share your master's joy!" (Matthew 25:21). Jesus told His followers, "Whoever is faithful in very little is also faithful in much" (Luke 16:10). David is a great example of faithfulness despite humble beginnings.

As president of Tennessee Temple University, I often meet dynamic students who come to campus with amazing abilities and communication skills. These students sometimes dream of becoming spiritual leaders who impact thousands and even millions of people with their faith. But the true test of their future greatness is whether those students are willing to help feed the homeless or visit someone in a nursing home. I can always predict that those students who are willing to stay faithful in a small aspect of service will be used in big ways by God to reach many people throughout their lives.

In the example of David, we see several traits that led to his later prominence. *First, David was faithful to watch his father's sheep.* As the youngest son of seven brothers, David was given the work the other six despised. David's three oldest brothers served in the military. That created a need in the family business, so "David kept going back and forth from Saul to tend his father's flock in Bethlehem" (1 Samuel 17:15). David left his job as a musician for the nation's top leader to watch sheep. Most people would have complained about this obvious demotion. However, we are simply told that David did it. There is no mention of complaints or excuses.

Second, David was faithful in the little things. There was nothing newsworthy about keeping sheep. The only time your name would be mentioned was when something went wrong and a sheep was lost. God wants us to be faithful in the insignificant so He can trust us with the magnificent. David was faithful in the menial things outside the spotlight. You might start by making pizzas or waiting tables at a low-paying job, but God often uses such experiences to test and prepare us for future situations in life. How you perform in your current context now will determine how God will use you in the future.

Third, David was faithful to obey his parents. This is sometimes not a popular message, but the truth is that respect for parents plays an important part in all of your future endeavors. You will never be used to the fullest extent that God wants until you learn to honor your mom and dad. The Bible tells us, "Children, obey your parents in the Lord, because this is right. Honor your father and mother—which is the first commandment with a promise—that it may go well with you and that you may have a long life in the land" (Ephesians 6:1–3). Another verse instructs, "Children, obey your parents in everything, for this is pleasing in the Lord" (Colossians 3:20). Following the leadership of your parents is an important step as you follow the leadership of God.

Notice what happened when David was faithful to care for his father's sheep. His father, the one who sent David to the pasture in the first place, later sent him to the battlefield. David was obedient in the little things, and God rewarded him with something greater. Soon David was headed to battle.

Fourth, David was faithful to run with the right people. "Israel and the Philistines lined up in battle formation facing each other. David left his supplies in the care of the quartermaster and ran to the battle line" (1 Samuel 17:21–22). He desired to stand with people who were standing for God. David was eager to stand with the right crowd for the right cause. He would later write, "I am a friend to all who fear You, to those who keep Your precepts" (Psalm 119:63).

For better or worse, you become like the people you regularly spend time with. If I want to know what your life is like, all I need to do is spend a few minutes with the people you spend the most time with. It is vital that we choose to invest in some relationships with like-minded people with a passion for God.

Fifth, David was also a leader among those who stood for God. When the crowd would not stand up, David stood. There are times when even the right crowd is tempted to make a wrong choice. In those situations someone has to take a stand. There must be someone to champion God's cause when we are faced with a difficult decision or temptation. When Israel failed to confront Goliath and his army, David made the tough choice to do something about it. He said, "Just who is this uncircumcised Philistine that he should defy the armies of the living God?" (1 Samuel 17:26).

You are given the opportunity to choose how you will respond to life's challenges. The army of Israel wasted forty days in indecision. David responded at the time he recognized the situation. Your spiritual giants will not go away until you do something about them.

Heroes Look Forward to the Reward

Heroes also spot the potential reward for defeating spiritual giants. In David's case, he asked what the person who killed Goliath would receive (1 Samuel 17:26). He was told, "The king will make the man who kills him very rich and will give him his daughter. The king will also make the household of that man's father exempt from paying taxes in Israel" (17:25).

There are great benefits for those who stand up for God. Jesus called our spiritual benefits *the abundant life:* "A thief comes only to steal and to kill and to destroy. I have come that they may have life and have it in abundance" (John 10:10). God honors obedience.

Heroes are not rewarded only in this world; they are also rewarded in the next life. Jesus said, "Look! I am coming quickly, and My reward is with Me to repay each person according to what he has done" (Revelation 22:12).

David held a different view of life from those around him. He saw the potential and *then* the problem. The army saw the problem and missed the potential. There is a big difference! Paul knew the difference and left these words of encouragement:

- "I am able to do all things through Him who strengthens me" (Philippians 4:13).
- "No, in all these things we are more than victorious through Him who loved us" (Romans 8:37).

- "What then are we to say about these things? If God is for us, who is against us?" (Romans 8:31).

The army saw Goliath. David saw God. The army saw the problem. David saw the power of God. David also recognized that his own power would not win the victory. He understood that it is "'Not by strength or by might, but by My Spirit,' says the LORD of Hosts" (Zechariah 4:6).

We cannot evaluate a situation in terms of only what is seen. If David had evaluated his situation in terms of only the human element, he would never have challenged Goliath. What is observable is real, but it is not the ultimate reality. Behind what we see is an all-powerful God. "Now faith is the reality of what is hoped for, the proof of what is not seen" (Hebrews 11:1). We are called to "walk by faith, not by sight" (2 Corinthians 5:7). Faith involves a willingness to put yourself in a position where if God doesn't come through, *you* are through. If your plans are not big enough that they will fail without God's intervention, *make bigger plans!*

Moses Faced Giants and Won

David was neither the first nor the last to face giants in his life. He and the Israelites were in God's Promised Land because of another unlikely risk-taker—Moses. Moses' giant was not a Philistine. Moses faced Pharaoh, the ruler of Egypt, the most powerful nation of his generation. He had been raised as an Egyptian, but later left his elite social standing to identify with his own people, the people of Israel. "By faith Moses, when he had grown up, refused

51

to be called the son of Pharaoh's daughter and chose to suffer with the people of God rather than to enjoy the short-lived pleasure of sin. For he considered reproach for the sake of the Messiah to be greater wealth than the treasures of Egypt, since his attention was on the reward. By faith he left Egypt behind, not being afraid of the king's anger, for he persevered, as one who sees Him who is invisible" (Hebrews 11:24–27).

The Old Testament includes information about Moses' early struggles. On one occasion Moses decided to confront an Egyptian worker who was physically abusing an Israelite slave. He tried to right injustices toward his people by taking matters into his own hands. In the process he killed the slavemaster and fled the nation as a fugitive. At forty years old Moses ran to save his own life and disappeared into obscurity.

A pastor named D. L. Moody once summarized the life of Moses in three phases. Moses spent the first forty years of his life learning he was a *somebody*. He "was learned in all the wisdom of the Egyptians, and was mighty in words and deeds" (Acts 7:22 NKJV). He then spent the next forty years learning he was a *nobody*. "Moses said to God, 'Who am I that I should go to Pharaoh, and that I should bring the children of Israel out of Egypt?'" (Exodus 3:11 NKJV). Then, Moses spent the final forty years of his life discovering *what God can do with a nobody*.[5] It was only then that he succeeded in making a true difference.

During the obscurity of Moses' second phase of his life, he learned the same lessons as David. His education came in the same form of watching sheep in the middle of nowhere. There Moses learned to lead sheep, which would prepare him to lead God's people. He endured years of work that no one but God noticed.

His new status as part of a shepherding family also meant *he had to learn how to live under authority.* Raised as the son of Pharaoh's daughter, Moses lived with people serving him. Now he was the servant. It would have been especially difficult for him to obey his father-in-law when he was asked to care for the sheep because shepherding was considered one of the worst possible jobs for Egyptians (see Genesis 46:34).

One of the most important lessons Moses learned during those desert years was *how to stand alone.* It was a skill he would regularly need during the most productive phase of his life. Moses had to stand alone against Pharaoh and his magicians in the palace. He had to stand alone against the leaders of Israel. Moses often had to stand alone through a series of rebellions among those he led from Egypt.

Between ages forty and eighty, Moses also learned to *look beyond his problems to God's power.* It was God's power that led Israel from Egypt. In the only psalm attributed to Moses, he began with the words, "Lord, You have been our refuge in every generation. Before the mountains were born, before You gave birth to the earth and the world, from eternity to eternity, You are God" (Psalm 90:1–2). Because Moses learned who God was, he was able to put Pharaoh and his other problems into perspective.

It was his relationship with God that enabled him to trust God completely and move forward, even when he was not entirely sure where the journey would take him. In the desert Moses learned to walk by faith rather than by sight.

Moses and the Next Generation

Moses used the lessons he learned to take on his spiritual giants and succeed. He also communicated those principles to the generation that followed. He wanted those he served and led to succeed as well. While Moses led an entire nation of people, there was one person he invested in above all others. It was a young man named Joshua, who would later become the next leader of God's people.

For much of his life, Joshua was simply described as the servant of Moses. As his servant, Joshua learned to be faithful in little things and accept the menial tasks that would be left to him in a secondary role. Again, this preparation was God's path for Joshua's later leadership. Jesus affirmed this attitude when He said, "If anyone wants to be first, he must be last of all and servant of all" (Mark 9:35) and that, "The greatest among you will be your servant" (Matthew 23:11).

Joshua started as part of a slave family in Egypt. He had to learn how to deal with the leadership of the Egyptian rulers who controlled much of his life. When Israel escaped from Egypt, many Israelites struggled to follow any other leadership, including Moses. In contrast, Joshua used his freedom to serve Moses, accepting the new authority God had placed in his life.

We know little about Joshua's friends, but we do know that one of his closest friends besides Moses was a guy named Caleb. When God encouraged Israel to move into the Promised Land, and the majority report of the spies discouraged them, Caleb was the one other person who stood with Joshua for what was right.

Later, when Joshua led the nation, his exploits for God made the list of God's heroes in the New Testament (see Hebrews 11:30). He saw what God had done for Israel in Egypt and was prepared to trust God with his future. For forty years Joshua trusted God and followed His leadership through the wilderness. When he later led Israel, by faith he led them from one victory to another.

His success was based on the Word of God and following God completely: "This book of instruction must not depart from your mouth; you are to recite it day and night, so that you may carefully observe everything written in it. For then you will prosper and succeed in whatever you do" (Joshua 1:8).

What about You?

God continues to seek heroes who will lead His battles today. Are you ready? Let's review what it takes:

1. Are you faithful in the little things so God can give you larger responsibilities down the road?
2. Do you accept responsibility for small tasks, even if no one notices but God?
3. Have you learned to honor and respect authority, including your parents?
4. Have you selected an inner circle of friends who will help you grow in your walk with God?

5. Have you chosen to stand for what is right even if it means standing alone?

6. Are you looking beyond your problems to God's power to solve your problems?

7. Will you trust God and move forward, even if you are not entirely sure which way to turn? Can you follow God walking by faith rather than sight?

Maybe as you reviewed the above questions, you uncovered areas to improve in your own life. Only you and God know what you need to do to become one of God's heroes in this generation. The question for you is, "What do you have to change to follow God 100 percent?"

⊠ THINK ABOUT IT ⊠

1. Long before David fought Goliath, there was a maturing process in his life. What were the areas in which David had to grow? In what areas is God calling you to be faithful? Which of those areas do you find most challenging?

2. What was God trying to teach Moses during his forty years in the wilderness? How do you think God is trying to teach you a similar lesson in your life?

3. When Moses led Israel out of Egypt to the Promised Land, God chose a route that would take them through the wilderness. According to Deuteronomy 8:2–5, how did God use the wilderness to prepare Israel for the

challenges they would face? What kinds of things delayed Israel's spiritual growth in the wilderness? Which of these are areas with which you also struggle?

4. Into what kind of life was Joshua born? How would you feel if you had been born into that situation? How did Joshua choose to use his new freedom? What was the key to Joshua's ultimate success? What can you apply from his example?

5. The Bible often reminds us that humility comes before honor (see James 4:10). As you review the list at the end of this chapter, how are you doing? What is the top area for you to work on at this point in your life?

Chapter 4

MISSION POSSIBLE

Depend on God's Power in Your Life

To the casual observer, the meeting was much like many others that had come before it. A group of Christians had gathered to hear the guest speaker, a well-known evangelist and Bible teacher of his time. While he spoke for some time, it was one line in his message that is best remembered. It is remembered because of its impact on one young man in the audience that night. It gave him a purpose and changed his life forever.

Today not many Christians are familiar with the ministry of Henry Varley. Still fewer remember his sermon from that night. At one point in his message, he made a statement: "The world has yet to see what God will do with a man who is fully and wholly consecrated to him."

Those words cut deep into the heart of a person named Dwight Lyman Moody that evening. Previously his goal in life had been to become a successful businessman and make money. Suddenly that was no longer enough. "By the grace of God," Moody said to himself and to God, "I will be that man."

D. L. Moody was true to his word and gave his life to serve God. He helped reach thousands of people with the message of Christ's love through his speaking and writing; he started Moody Bible Institute, Moody Publishers, and several additional ministries that have made an impact in numerous nations around the world and still continue today.

Toward the end of his life, Moody met informally with a few close friends. It was a time of reflecting on where they had been and what they had seen God do in their lives. In the course of the conversation, Moody mentioned the meeting with Henry Varley and the commitment he had made that night. Then, knowing himself better than anyone else in that room, Moody confessed, "I was not that man. The world has *yet* to see what God can do through one life completely dedicated to His cause."[6]

If God Wanted to Change the World

If God really wanted to change our world today, how would He do it? God has every resource available in the universe. Yet God is changing the world today through a process. He is using people like you and me to communicate the message of Christ's love. Jesus outlined this plan when He said,

All authority has been given to Me in heaven
and on earth. Go, therefore, and make disciples
of all nations, baptizing them in the name
of the Father and of the Son and of the Holy
Spirit, teaching them to observe everything
I have commanded you. And remember,
I am with you always, to the end of the age.
(Matthew 28:18–20)

Without question, Jesus expects us to speak with passion about Him with other people. The book of Acts in the New Testament begins with the promise of Jesus to His followers: "But you will receive power when the Holy Spirit has come upon you, and you will be My witnesses in Jerusalem, in all Judea and Samaria, and to the ends of the earth" (Acts 1:8). Jesus promised the spiritual *power* they needed to accomplish the spiritual *purpose* He had given them.

When did they get that power? Acts 2 describes the coming of the Holy Spirit to the early Christians, initiating a new age in the plan of God. Their power came when the Holy Spirit came, and they boldly began to tell "the magnificent acts of God" (2:11). Before the day was through, three thousand people joined their movement. The rest of Acts shares the story of the incredible growth of early Christianity as people spread the message of Christ across the Roman Empire and beyond.

Some people today are waiting for a supernatural experience before they begin sharing their faith in Christ. Yet they fail to realize that the Holy Spirit who accomplished so much through those early Christians is already at work in their lives. "For we were all baptized

61

by one Spirit into one body—whether Jews or Greeks, whether slaves or free—and we were all made to drink of one Spirit" (1 Corinthians 12:13). There is no reason for Christians to wait to obey God. We already have God's power at work within us.

We have the power of God that Jesus promised the early Christ-followers, but there is more. We also have the resurrection power of God at work in our lives by the indwelling presence of Christ. *Indwelling* simply means that "His power" lives within us. When Paul prayed for the Ephesians, he referred to "the immeasurable greatness of His power to us who believe, according to the working of His vast strength. He demonstrated this power in the Messiah by raising Him from the dead and seating Him at His right hand in the heavens" (Ephesians 1:19–20).

All of the information we need to communicate the Good News of Jesus effectively is in the Bible. I find that the more Scripture I use when I share Christ with others, the more likely they are to respond to God's grace. God's Word tells us, "For the word of God is living and effective and sharper than any two-edged sword, penetrating as far as to divide soul, spirit, joints, and marrow; it is a judge of the ideas and thoughts of the heart" (Hebrews 4:12).

The Bible has a supernatural way of breaking through the barriers we raise between ourselves and God to deal with the core issue. As Paul explained to his friend Timothy, the Scriptures are "able to instruct you for salvation through faith in Christ Jesus" (2 Timothy 3:15).

I like to use the word **BIBLE** as an acrostic to remind me of the impact the Bible can have in my life. The Bible:

Brightens my day.

The psalmist wrote, "Your word is a lamp for my feet and a light on my path" (Psalm 119:105).

Instructs my life.

"Make my steps steady through Your promise; don't let sin dominate me" (119:133).

Builds me up.

Paul told the Ephesian church leaders, "And now I commit you to God and to the message of His grace, which is able to build you up and to give you an inheritance among all who are sanctified" (Acts 20:32).

Liberates me from sin and Satan.

Jesus said, "You will know the truth, and the truth will set you free" (John 8:32). The psalmist noted, "I will walk freely in an open place because I seek Your precepts" (Psalm 119:45).

Everlasting, forever.

"LORD, Your word is forever; it is firmly fixed in heaven" (119:89).

There is nothing more exciting, illuminating, transforming, convicting, and confronting than the Word of God. It will set your life on fire. It can turn your life upside down. It will make you the person God is calling you to be. If you spend thirty days of quality time reading the Bible, you will experience something only God can give you, and you'll never want to let that go. It is essential if you really want to be a world-changer for God.

However, it is equally important that we give credibility to our message by living out God's Word through our lives. Jesus said, "Let your light shine before men, so that they may see your good works and give glory to your Father in heaven" (Matthew 5:16). Paul reminded the Corinthians, "You yourselves are our letter, written on our hearts, recognized and read by everyone, since it is plain that you are Christ's letter, produced by us, not written with ink but with the Spirit of the living God; not on stone tablets but on tablets that are hearts of flesh" (2 Corinthians 3:2–3).

You are the only Bible many people will ever read. Before people will read the Bible for themselves, they will read the Bible of your life. If your life translation speaks to their hearts, they will be drawn to the written Word and be more receptive to God's truth when it is shared.

Paul: God's Pattern for Us

Paul has been described as one of history's greatest Christian leaders. Without question, he was the greatest missionary of his age and an example for every missionary since then. Even today, world mission leaders look to Paul's experiences and teachings to identify principles for modern outreach strategies. God used him as the most influential person to share Christ with the Greco-Roman culture of his generation.

At times when Paul's words are taken out of context, some have thought of him as arrogant. Why? When Paul wrote to his protégé, Timothy, he commanded him to follow his example in church leadership efforts: "And what you have heard from me in the presence of many witnesses, commit to faithful men who will be able to teach others also" (2 Timothy 2:2).

In another letter Paul highlighted his own life and ministry as a guide to help the Philippians know how to live. "Do what you have learned and received and heard and seen in me, and the God of peace will be with you" (Philippians 4:9). Paul even had the audacity once to write, "Be imitators of me, as I also am of Christ" (1 Corinthians 11:1).

However, there was never a question in Paul's mind whether he could live the Christian life in his own strength. He shared his personal frustrations in one letter, sharing, "For I know that nothing good lives in me, that is, in my flesh. For the desire to do what is good is with me, but there is no ability to do it. For I do not do the good that I want to do, but I practice the evil that I do not want to do" (Romans 7:18–19). Paul knew his experience would also be the experience of others who tried to live passionately for Christ. Our human, sinful nature makes it impossible in our own strength.

By definition, to be a Christian is to live like Christ. Throughout history, only one person has ever successfully lived the life of Christ—Jesus Himself. That is why Paul said, "But thanks be to God, who gives us the victory through our Lord Jesus Christ!" (1 Corinthians 15:57). Understanding and consistently applying that principle is the foundation for success in your spiritual development. Only as you do that can you "be steadfast, immovable, always excelling in the Lord's work, knowing that your labor in the Lord is not in vain" (15:58).

Paul revealed the key to living the Christian life in his earliest letter. He wrote, "I no longer live, but Christ lives in me. The life I now live in the flesh, I live by faith in the Son of God, who loved me and gave Himself for me" (Galatians 2:20). Several hundred years ago Henry Scougal described the Christian life in a book he called *The Life of God in the Soul of Men*. That is the key— Christ living his life through you.

It sounds easy, but it's far from it. During tough times it is easy to quit. Paul understood that part of God's purpose in his life was to help him stand in times of trouble. He told Timothy, "But I received mercy because of this, so that in me, the worst of them, Christ Jesus might demonstrate the utmost patience as an example to those who would believe in Him for eternal life." (1 Timothy 1:16). Paul described himself as the first in a series of patterns that would demonstrate what God could do in a person's life. When we get discouraged and think living for God is impossible, we can look to the life of Paul as a positive example to follow.

Notice that Paul used the word "first" (KJV) describing himself as a *pattern* for the Christian life. This implies there would be other patterns to follow. Certainly Paul anticipated that Timothy would also be a pattern God would use to encourage others to live for Him. Today you and I are the patterns God has placed in this generation. When people look at our lives, they should see what God can do when we passionately follow Him.

Sharing Your Story

Your spiritual story (sometimes called your personal testimony) often serves as the most effective way to share Christ. Many people don't care about Jesus until they see the difference He makes in your life. But even if they see the change, they may not know what caused it until you take the time to tell them. Your spiritual story works best when you combine the power of *declaring* the Good News of Christ with the power of *demonstrating* Christ in your life.

A testimony is an expression of what God has done in your life. Normally it focuses on your initial change or conversion, although it also includes how your life is now different as a result of Christ's work within you. Sometimes sharing your spiritual story will be only one of several steps in the extended process of helping people follow Christ. At other times, your story may be the starting point for a life-changing conversation, even to the point that you can be the one to help another person cross the line of faith to choose Christ as the leader and forgiver of his or her life.

As you prepare to communicate how Christ has changed your life, begin by praying for wisdom (James 1:5–6). Be as focused as possible, but also realize that only

God can perform the miracle of a changed life. We serve as His representatives in the process.

In three places in the book of Acts, the apostle Paul shared how Christ changed his life (Acts 22:1–21; 24:10–21; 26:2–23). Comparing these accounts reveals that Paul had a plan he used to communicate his faith. He began by briefly describing his life *before* his conversion. Then he shared what happened *during* the time he came to faith in Christ. Finally he described the difference in his life *after* his conversion. The same process can easily be adapted as you develop a game plan to share your faith.

Be positive as you share how Christ has changed you. You can do this by emphasizing the changes reflected in your *new* life rather than the failings of your *old* life. Also, emphasize the good things you have in Christ rather than the things you lost or gave up by becoming a Christian. Every life change involves gains and losses, but the life change that takes place when we trust Christ has far more gains than losses.

It is also helpful to focus on a single theme in your spiritual story rather than revealing every detail of your life. When you describe your experience in the context of loneliness, forgiveness, or a search for personal fulfillment, people with similar needs will readily identify with your experience. If you try to identify the hundreds of changes that took place when you began to follow Jesus, your story will lose focus and the interest of those who listen.

As you describe your life before Christ, your purpose is to build a bridge between yourself and the other person. Include enough detail to enable the other person to identify with your experience, but be careful not to glamorize the past. The ultimate desire is to help people understand that a life of joy is found only in Christ (John 10:10).

The climax of sharing your spiritual story should be an answer to the question, "What does Christ mean to you today?" There are many ways to answer this question, but it is best to mention only two or three things that are most significant. Emphasize what is most meaningful in your life without sounding like a commercial. Your testimony is an expression of what God has done in your life. It does not have to be glamorous, but it should at least be interesting.

It is also helpful to physically write or type out your testimony. Through writing, you can determine how to best introduce and end your story and allow appropriate balance between the various parts of your spiritual journey. You can also pause to add Bible verses that connect with your story. Think of your spiritual story as a movie. It should include a compelling beginning, a middle section that highlights the essential story line of your journey, and an ending that leaves people with a very real sense of hope in the midst of a difficult situation.

If you write out your story, you'll notice that it may take more than one draft to make it really stand out. Look at it critically from the perspective of the listener. Are you using clichés, negative statements, stereotypes, or words many people will not understand? Is your testimony personal enough that others will relate to you? It is your story and must be true to who you are, but remember that you are communicating to impact others. Emphasize only what someone else needs to hear.

If you type your spiritual story, you can use the word count tool in your computer program to check how long it is. The typical newscaster reads the news at a rate of 160 words per minute. This means a three- to five-hundred word testimony would take two to three minutes to share. Remember, shorter is better. You may even want to develop different versions for various situations, such as a one-minute version, five-minute version, and ten-minute version.

The most frightening part for most people is actually sharing it! Public speaking is considered one of our culture's greatest fears. To help, ask one or two of your friends to listen to your story and give you some feedback on how to make it better. You can even do this with those who do not follow Christ and share your faith at the same time you practice!

These are helpful tips. However, the most important thing is to share with people. Even if your story is not perfect, God can and often does use your input to lead people to consider following Jesus. As the Bible encourages, make the most of every opportunity.

What Does God Want to Do in Your Life?

The guidelines I have outlined above will help you prepare your personal testimony as an effective way to share what God has done in your life. However, these steps are effective only if God is actually *doing* something in your life. God has a purpose for you. If you let

Him, He will accomplish that purpose. Paul described that purpose as being "conformed to the image of His Son" (Romans 8:29). He wants you to be like Jesus.

But is this even possible? In one sense, we will not become like Christ no matter how hard we try. However, our goal is to become increasingly Christ-like. That means that today we strive to become more Christ-like than yesterday. Wake up tomorrow and repeat the process.

The Bible promises us that God is up to the task:

- "He who calls you is faithful, who also will do it" (1 Thessalonians 5:24).
- "I am sure of this, that He who started a good work in you will carry it on to completion until the day of Christ Jesus" (Philippians 1:6).
- "For it is God who is working in you, enabling you both to will and to act for His good purpose" (Philippians 2:13).
- "For we are His creation—created in Christ Jesus for good works, which God prepared ahead of time so that we should walk in them" (Ephesians 2:10).

There is no question about it. God is ready, willing, and able to take on the task of transforming you into the image of Christ.

When you look at your life, can you see the changes God is making? If not, you might want to take a closer look at your life. God wants to transform you and use you. As you commit your life to Him, you invite God to demonstrate what He can do in your life.

Paul reminded Timothy, "Now in a large house there are not only gold and silver bowls, but also those of wood and earthenware, some for special use, some for ordinary. So if anyone purifies himself from these things, he will be a special instrument, set apart, useful to the Master, prepared for every good work" (2 Timothy 2:20–21). God's desire is for you and me to come to Him with a clean heart so He can use us to change the lives of others in your life, your community, and around the world.

⇥ THINK ABOUT IT ⇤

1. "The world has yet to see what God will do with a man who is fully and wholly consecrated to him." Those words are a great challenge still today. Are you prepared to be that "one life completely dedicated to His cause"? What could God do through your life if you were all He meant you to be?

2. Someone has said, "We cannot do the work of God without the power of God!" Have you tried serving God without relying on God's power? What happened? What is stopping you from walking in the power of God's Spirit daily?

3. The Bible is another source of the power of God (Romans 1:16). How much of the Bible are you injecting into your life? If you memorized just one verse a week, you would know fifty-two more verses a year from now.

What kind of commitment to Scripture knowledge are you prepared to make?

4. One of God's purposes in Paul's life was for him to live as a pattern of the Christian life for others to follow. Could that be a purpose of God for your life also? Read Matthew 5:16 and 2 Corinthians 3:2–3. What parts of your life cause others to glorify your Father in heaven? What must change?

5. This chapter includes guidelines for writing your personal testimony. Have you written out your spiritual story? Take the challenge to write it out and share it with at least one friend as soon as possible.

Chapter 5

STAND FIRM

Determine Your Values (or Others Will)

In my work I speak to thousands of high school and college students each year. I speak at college campuses and some of the largest youth camps, rallies, and conferences in the country. While I count it a great privilege to speak to these students, I also take time to listen to what they are saying.

Many teenagers tell me, "There is no way I can live the victorious life as a teenager. The peer pressure is too tough. The temptation is too great. The circumstances I face are impossible."

In response I remind them, "You can live victoriously *if* you have an intimate relationship with Jesus Christ." The Bible promises, "The One who is in you is greater than the one who is in the world" (1 John 4:4). According to the apostle Paul, "In all these things we are more than victorious through Him who loved us" (Romans 8:37). When you understand some basic principles and apply them consistently, you can experience consistent victory in your life.

Daniel faced every major challenge faced by students in America today. Yet he was able to rise above his circumstances and take a stand for God when it really counted. His name was changed in an attempt to transfer his allegiance from his God to the gods of the Babylonians, but Daniel continued to pursue God's purpose in his life. He was exposed to a school that would have trained him in values that opposed his spiritual beliefs, but he continued to look to God to shape his values. He could function within his culture, but when social pressures pushed him to compromise his core values, Daniel resisted.

A lot of students start well, but struggle to maintain high standards for the long haul. For instance, when Christian teenagers begin a new dating relationship, they know their physical boundaries. But as the relationship begins pushing the edges of those boundaries, those boundaries have a tendency to slide. The shift may start as a small compromise, but given time, the boundaries disappear. Before long, the relationship determines the standards rather than the standards determining the extent of the relationship.

One key to living without compromise is to learn how to take your stand when it is time to be counted. Daniel took his stand and continued to pray to God three times a day even when prayer became punishable by death.

David took his stand before Goliath when it was time to be counted. Shadrach, Meshach, and Abednego stood for God in a fiery furnace when it was time to be counted. Esther stood before the king to save her people when it was time to be counted. Moses stood with God and the people of Israel when it was time to be counted. And God continues to look for people who will take their stand and be counted today.

All of these leaders in the Bible stood for God at crucial turning points in their lives, but they were only able to do that because they had made a lifestyle decision much earlier. If you want to be the kind of person who can stand for God in a crisis, you need to learn how to stand for God right now. Long before Daniel chose to pray boldly after the ban on prayer, he was standing for God in making smaller decisions about what he would eat.

Daniel's Diet for God

Early in his Babylonian experience, Daniel was offered food that he felt was in conflict with his spiritual beliefs. The Bible is not completely clear about what specific foods were served, but "Daniel determined that he would not defile himself with the king's food or with the wine he drank" (Daniel 1:8). The foods probably included nonkosher meats or meat dishes made from animals the Jewish law did not allow God's people to eat.

Having decided he would not eat what had been provided by the king, Daniel spoke to his leader and explained the situation. Initially the Babylonian officials opposed his request. They saw nothing wrong with the food provided. In contrast to Daniel, they believed it was a healthy diet. So Daniel proposed a short-term test to see which diet was more effective.

Daniel suggested, "Please test your servants for 10 days. Let us be given vegetables to eat and water to drink. Then examine our appearance and the appearance of the young men who are eating the king's food, and deal with your servants based on what you see" (1:12–13). Daniel was confident he would be better off following God's revealed truth. He was willing to adopt a vegetarian diet for a week and a half to demonstrate what God does when you stand for Him, even when it means standing against the culture.

The Babylonian officials agreed to the test, and as Daniel expected, he and his friends turned out healthier than the others (1:15). Beyond the normal positive consequences one might expect from a healthy diet, "God gave these four young men knowledge and understanding in every kind of literature and wisdom. Daniel also understood visions and dreams of every kind" (1:17). At the end of the three years, Daniel and his friends were examined by the king: "In every matter of wisdom and understanding that the king consulted them about, he found them 10 times better than all the diviner-priests and mediums in his entire kingdom" (1:20).

Daniel took a stand to be counted in what seemed to be a little thing. This habit of standing for God was highly developed by the time prayer became illegal in his town. Daniel made a commitment as a teenager that he lived out all of his life. He never crossed back over the line to give up on his beliefs.

Sixty Years Later

Around sixty years later, a new king named Darius came to power. According to Daniel, "Darius decided to appoint 120 satraps over the kingdom, stationed throughout the realm, and over them three administrators, including Daniel" (6:1–2). Daniel was promoted above his peers, and they became jealous of his success.

You may run into the same situation. As God blesses you, others will want what you have without making the kind of commitment to God you have made. Jealousy and criticism will be the natural result. Occasionally that jealousy can lead to someone actively seeking your harm. We find this extreme situation in the life of Daniel.

However, there was a problem when Daniel's enemies decided to find fault in him and have him removed from office. They could find no dirt on him. Not a single scandal. Why? Daniel had an excellent spirit (6:3–4).

Many people who claim to follow Christ today are too self-focused to have a right attitude. The Bible says, "Everyone should look out not only for his own interests, but also for the interests of others" (Philippians 2:4). Daniel understood that principle. He had an excellent attitude.

Attitude will always determine your altitude! Paul had the right attitude. He had an *I can* attitude: "I am able to do all things through Him who strengthens me" (4:13). We need more next-generation Christian leaders to become *I can* Christians. As Luke wrote, "For nothing will be impossible with God" (Luke 1:37).

In Daniel's situation, "The administrators and satraps, therefore, kept trying to find a charge against Daniel regarding the kingdom. But they could find no charge or corruption, for he was trustworthy, and no negligence or corruption was found in him" (Daniel 6:4). They could find no corruption. Daniel had given 100 percent to all God had called him to do, whether it was in his work or in his worship.

Daniel was faithful to God first. Then he was faithful to his position and title in the kingdom. He knew God had placed him there to be a source of light for God's honor. While the Bible never claims Daniel lived a perfect life, it also never records a single major sin he committed.

The only thing Daniel's opponents could find wrong with him was his devotion to God. Very convicting, isn't it? If I asked five of your friends what they admired most about you, would they say it was your devotion to God? If not, what *would* they say? Daniel was known as a person devoted to God even by those who didn't believe in his God.

Guilty of Living a Godly Life

When you take a stand for God, you have a supernatural protection. Earlier in his life we are told, "God had granted Daniel favor and compassion from the chief official" (Daniel 1:9). Daniel had a choice to make early on: eat meat and drink wine or be killed. When he took an uncompromising stand, God provided supernatural protection.

Jesus said, "No one who puts his hand to the plow and looks back is fit for the kingdom of God" (Luke 9:62). But when you take an uncompromising stand, even if you stand by yourself, you are promised by God that He will intervene and take care of you when the going gets tough. When Daniel said, "I'm not going to do it," his boss did not get mad and kill him. The Bible says Daniel was well respected by his boss. "When a man's ways please the LORD, He makes even his enemies to be at peace with him" (Proverbs 16:7).

I think I know why people will be at peace with you. Even enemies respect somebody who stands for their beliefs. We live in a culture in which people say one thing in private and something completely contradictory in public. So when a person boldly stands for his or her convictions, people notice.

Daniel had an uncommon standard and an unearthly protection. Fast-forward to later in Daniel's life. He was told, "If you don't quit praying, you'll be thrown into a room full of hungry lions." What would you have done in that situation? A lot of Christians would still have prayed, but only in secret.

When Daniel heard their threat, he did the unthinkable. He knelt in front of an open window and prayed! God had provided for Daniel for seven decades, and Daniel wasn't about to turn his back on Him now.

Daniel knew the likely consequences of his actions before he knelt to pray, but he did it anyway. As soon as his enemies documented Daniel's violation of the new law, they brought their case to the king and had Daniel arrested. "As soon as the king heard this, he was very displeased; he set his mind on rescuing Daniel and made every effort until sundown to deliver him" (Daniel 6:14).

As soon as he realized Daniel in good conscience could not abide by this new regulation, Darius knew he had been tricked into signing the law. He spent the rest of the day trying to change the situation, but he had no way to escape the consequences of his actions. Under the law of the Medes and Persians, "no edict or ordinance the king establishes can be changed" (6:15). As the sentence was executed, all Darius could say to Daniel was, "May your God, whom you serve continually, rescue you!" (6:16). There was nothing more the king could do. Daniel's only hope was God. But God was the only hope Daniel needed.

How Well Do You Sleep?

That night Daniel slept like a baby in a den of hungry lions. As the lions saw someone being lowered into their den that evening, they looked forward to dinner. But when they saw it was Daniel and realized he was protected by angels, they decided they were not that hungry after all.

The one person who didn't sleep well that night was King Darius. We're told, "Then the king went to his palace and spent the night fasting. No diversions were brought to him, and he could not sleep" (6:18). As morning began to dawn, "The king got up and hurried to the lions' den. When he reached the den, he cried out in anguish to Daniel. 'Daniel, servant of the living God,' the king said, 'has your God whom you serve continually been able to rescue you from the lions?'" (6:19–20).

Had Daniel's accusers realized what the next day would bring, it is doubtful *they* would have slept well. When the king pulled Daniel out of the lions' den, the lions were still hungry. "The king then gave the command, and those men who had maliciously accused Daniel were brought and thrown into the lions' den" (6:24).

How could Daniel take a stand for God under such incredible pressure? He knew he served an awesome God, a God whose Word was completely reliable. When he knelt before God in prayer, he began by saying, "Ah, Lord—the great and awe-inspiring God who keeps His gracious covenant with those who love Him and keep His commandments" (9:4). Daniel's God kept His covenant. God was not disappointed with Daniel because Daniel loved Him and kept His commandments.

The real question is whether God will be disappointed with you—or will you, like Daniel, take your stand when it is time to be counted?

◧ THINK ABOUT IT ◨

1. It's tough to live for God in our culture. What kind of challenges did Daniel face in Babylon that are similar to those you face today? Which of your challenges do you find easiest to deal with? Most difficult?

2. Sometimes it is possible to appeal to those in authority over us and change difficult situations. How did Daniel make his appeal? What did Daniel do to satisfy his leader's concerns without compromising his own convictions? How did Daniel's attitude help make his appeal successful?

3. What spiritual practices do you use to keep connected with God? Is there an area you are not practicing but feel you should? How would practicing that discipline help you grow as a Christian? What would be a reasonable first step to take this week to make that discipline a part of your Christian life?

4. When Daniel's critics looked for something wrong in his life, they had to attack his faith in God. How easy is it for your critics to find something wrong in your life? If it were illegal today to be a Christian, would there be enough evidence to convict you?

5. This chapter ends with two questions we all need to ask ourselves. In light of the way you are currently living your life, will God be disappointed with you? Will you, like Daniel, take your stand when it is time to be counted? What is one area of life in which you could take a stand for God right now?

Chapter 6

KEEP TRUSTING GOD

Distinguish Your Life by Your Faith

The single most important discipline in the Christian life is trusting God: "Now without faith it is impossible to please God, for the one who draws near to Him must believe that He exists and rewards those who seek Him" (Hebrews 11:6). "But whoever doubts stands condemned if he eats, because his eating is not from faith, and everything that is not from faith is sin" (Romans 14:23). Great men and women of God are first and foremost always great men and women of faith.

Shadrach, Meshach, and Abednego were men of uncompromising faith. Even though they were captives in an alien land, they had risen to places of prominence in government. Life was good and they could afford to enjoy the best Babylon had to offer. But despite their success in life, they never forgot to honor God.

Then one day a memo crossed their desks from the palace. Nebuchadnezzar had decided to build a huge golden idol ninety feet tall and nine feet wide. Some scholars believe Nebuchadnezzar was trying to recreate something he had seen in one of his dreams. The idol would represent the power of the kingdom and his power as king. The new law of the kingdom was that every person must bow down and worship this new idol.

The consequences for breaking the new law were clear. Those who would not bow down to the idol would burn in a furnace. This created a problem for Shadrach, Meshach, and Abednego. They had chosen to live without compromise despite the beliefs of their employers. While there was often flexibility in the issues they faced each day, this law was required of everyone. But their allegiance to God came first. They could not and would not bow down to an idol, even if it cost them their jobs and even if it cost them their lives.

America's Idols

We don't have to worry about bowing down to a golden statue, but idols still distract people from God today. An idol is anything that becomes more important to you than God. It can be a car, a sport, a hobby, a job, money, or even a person. Whatever is more important to you than God is your idol.

The Christian life can be summed up in two words: Jesus first. Jesus said, "But seek first the kingdom of

God and His righteousness, and all these things will be provided for you" (Matthew 6:33). There are many things that can come between you and your God.

When Nebuchadnezzar issued his decree, it included a sense of urgency. He announced that when the music began to play, everybody should bow. Then he added, "But whoever does not fall down and worship will immediately be thrown into a furnace of blazing fire" (Daniel 3:6). There would be no time wasted on a trial. There was no concept of *innocent until proven guilty*. Those who would not bow would burn immediately.

Some people complain about how hard it is to live for God today. It can be tough, but none of us has faced what those three men faced.

Not only did the king issue a command complete with consequences, but throughout the land there was conformity: "Therefore, when all the people heard the sound of the horn, flute, zither, lyre, harp, and every kind of music, people of every nation and language fell down and worshiped the gold statue that King Nebuchadnezzar had set up" (3:7). All the people did bow—except for three! Can you imagine what that must have felt like—to stand with two friends while thousands of people around you bowed to an idol? One thing was certain—they were noticed!

The Conspiracy of the Ambitious

You can tell a lot about people by looking at the friends they have. Sometimes you can tell even more about people when you see their enemies. Shadrach, Meshach, and Abednego had the right kind of enemy.

It was reported by the king's leaders,

"May the king live forever. You as king have issued a decree that everyone who hears the sound of the horn, flute, zither, lyre, harp, drum, and every kind of music must fall down and worship the gold statue. Whoever does not fall down and worship will be thrown into a furnace of blazing fire. There are some Jews you have appointed to manage the province of Babylon: Shadrach, Meshach, and Abednego. These men have ignored you, the king; they do not serve your gods or worship the gold statue you have set up." (Daniel 3:9–12)

Under the terms of the law, those who refused to bow would be burned immediately. The fact that the king gave them a second chance indicates something of his regard for their leadership and character: "Nebuchadnezzar asked them, 'Shadrach, Meshach, and Abednego, is it true that you don't serve my gods or worship the gold statue I have set up?'" (3:14).

When Shadrach, Meshach, and Abednego arrived, the king tried to find a peaceful way to resolve the problem: "Now if you're ready, when you hear the sound of the horn, flute, zither, lyre, harp, drum, and every kind of music, fall down and worship the statue I made. But if you don't worship it, you will immediately be thrown into a furnace of blazing fire—and who is the god who can rescue you from my power?" (3:15). He was giving them a second chance to make the kind of compromise they could not make. And if you live for God without compromise today, you will likely be given multiple opportunities to turn back on your decision.

If you overcome your temptation the first time, it will come back more powerfully each time. Nebuchadnezzar tried to sound reasonable in his appeal, "Wait a minute. You don't understand. If you don't bow to me, let me tell you again what's going to happen. A little compromise on your part and we can all live happily ever after."

Isn't that how we are tempted? Satan whispers in your ear, "Hey, guys, I'm going to give you another chance. We're going to play the horns again and this time you're going to bow. And if you don't bow, fall down and worship the image which I have made, you will be cast into the midst of the fiery furnace immediately. Then what god will save you?"

Nebuchadnezzar was accurate in his argument until he challenged the God of Shadrach, Meshach, and Abednego. He had power over the three men, but not their God. He decided he was going to take on Shadrach, Meshach, and Abednego's God! And every time Satan tempts you to sin, he wants you to defy your God.

Men of Uncompromising Faith

When invited to deny their faith and worship a false god, Shadrach, Meshach, and Abednego refused to bow. Now when Nebuchadnezzar appealed for compromise on their part, they would not bend. Ultimately they would be forced to trust God in the midst of a fiery furnace. At that point, to everyone's surprise, they would not burn.

Through this ordeal, they demonstrated themselves to be men of uncompromising faith.

What made Shadrach, Meshach, and Abednego men of uncompromising faith? First, they were *courageous.* "Shadrach, Meshach, and Abednego replied to the king, 'Nebuchadnezzar, we don't need to give you an answer to this question'" (3:16). They responded to the king by pleading guilty right up front. They admitted their fault. What was their fault? "They followed one true God and no other. They would not bow."

What would you do in this situation? Sometimes it is easier to take a stand quickly, but what would happen the second time when faced with the choice and an influential leader says, "Bow or burn"?

A lot of us would be tempted to make excuses, "O King, you don't understand. The reason I didn't bow is that I have arthritis. It is not that I didn't want to bow, I just can't." Or some would bow and quietly pray, "Now, Lord, You know I still love You. I am not really bowing to this image to worship it. I am just bowing to the image to spend quality time praying to You. I know You understand because I can do more for You alive than dead."

It is easy to rationalize our compromises, isn't it? It is more convenient to give in to external pressure instead of obeying an internal principle. The reason Shadrach, Meshach, and Abednego never crossed the line into compromise was that at a very early age they made a promise to God. They had a principle in their hearts that they were not going to defile. They stayed as far from the world as they could, not as close as they could! They had already made up their minds.

Shadrach, Meshach, and Abednego chose to trust God regardless of the consequences. From a human perspective, they had basically said, "Go ahead and kill me." But they saw things from a different point of view:

> Shadrach, Meshach, and Abednego replied
> to the king, "Nebuchadnezzar, we don't need to
> give you an answer to this question. If the God
> we serve exists, then He can rescue us from the
> furnace of blazing fire, and He can rescue us
> from the power of you, the king. But even if He
> does not rescue us, we want you as king to know
> that we will not serve your gods or worship the
> gold statue you set up." (Daniel 3:16–18)

The early Christians faced similar challenges as the church began in Jerusalem. They were warned about preaching and offered a reprieve if they would tone things down a bit. All they had to do to live in peace was stop teaching in Jesus' name. Peter and John did not have to think long about their response. "But Peter and John answered them, 'Whether it's right in the sight of God for us to listen to you rather than to God, you decide; for we are unable to stop speaking about what we have seen and heard'" (Acts 4:19–20).

God wants us to serve and obey the authorities He has placed in our life as long as they do not cause us to disobey God's Word. The moment you are told, "Hey, now you're going to worship this false image that I've set up," God expects the response, "No, I will not!"

Sometimes this may enrage those who oppose us. In the case of Nebuchadnezzar, he passed sentence on these three objectors, and the sentence was executed immediately:

> He commanded some of the strongest soldiers in his army to tie up Shadrach, Meshach, and Abednego and throw them into the furnace of blazing fire. So these men, in their trousers, robes, head coverings, and other clothes, were tied up and thrown into the furnace of blazing fire. (Daniel 3:20–21)

The furnace was so hot the men who cast the Hebrews into the furnace died.

In spite of the circumstances they faced, Shadrach, Meshach, and Abednego trusted the promises of God. Isaiah wrote,

> Now this is what the Lord says—the One who created you, Jacob, and the One who formed you, Israel—"Do not fear, for I have redeemed you; I have called you by your name; you are Mine. I will be with you when you pass through the waters, and when you pass through the rivers, they will not overwhelm you. You will not be scorched when you walk through the fire, and the flame will not burn you. For I am the Lord your God, the Holy One of Israel, and your Savior." (Isaiah 43:1–3)

The Bible affirms God's promises to us during times of trouble in numerous places:

- "God is our refuge and strength, a helper who is always found in times of trouble. Therefore we will not be afraid, though the earth trembles and the mountains topple into the depths of the seas, though its waters roar and foam and the mountains quake with its turmoil" (Psalm 46:1–3).
- "Be strong and courageous; don't be terrified or afraid of them. For it is the LORD your God who goes with you; He will not leave you or forsake you" (Deuteronomy 31:6).
- "The LORD is for me; I will not be afraid. What can man do to me?" (Psalm 118:6).
- "The LORD is my light and my salvation—whom should I fear? The LORD is the stronghold of my life—of whom should I be afraid? When evildoers came against me to devour my flesh, my foes and my enemies stumbled and fell. Though an army deploy against me, my heart is not afraid; though war break out against me, still I am confident" (Psalm 27:1–3).

When God is on your side, you have nothing to fear! You don't have to fight your battles! He'll fight them for you! When God fights, He wins! "Then King Nebuchadnezzar jumped up in alarm. He said to his advisers, 'Didn't we throw three men, bound, into the fire?' 'Yes, of course, Your Majesty,' they replied to the king. He exclaimed, 'Look! I see four men, not tied, walking around in the fire unharmed; and the fourth looks like a son of the gods'" (Daniel 3:24–25).

The Reward of Faith

What a day it had been for the Hebrew trio! They began the day as respected leaders in Babylon and ended up in a fiery furnace. Through it all they trusted God with no guarantee He would intervene. As they were bound and carried to the furnace, their situation was hopeless.

But that is where faith in God really counts most. They had the faith of Abraham, "who, contrary to hope, in hope believed" (Romans 4:18 NKJV). Like Abraham, they, "did not waver in unbelief at God's promise, but [were] strengthened in [their] faith and gave glory to God, because [they were] fully convinced that what He had promised He was also able to perform" (4:20–21).

Only when they made it to the fire did God intervene. He allowed the fire to burn the ropes that bound them and turned the trio into a quartet. In doing so, God demonstrated an eternal principle regarding how He works in our lives. God does not deliver you *from* the fire, but He will deliver you while you are *in* the fire.

In the mid-twentieth century, God used a Scottish preacher named Duncan Campbell to bring revival to his country and others. His books and recordings continue to impact lives today. When Campbell spoke of revival, he called it, "The blessing of God." When he preached on revival, he would often say, "The blessing of God is God Himself."[6]

That is the reward of faith. That is what Shadrach, Meshach, and Abednego experienced in the midst of the fiery furnace. And that is what you will experience in the midst of your greatest difficulties if you continue to trust God regardless of the circumstances. As the Proverb observes, "Trust in the LORD with all your heart, and do not rely on your own understanding; think about Him in all your ways, and He will guide you on the right paths" (Proverbs 3:5–6).

But that's not the end of the story: "Nebuchadnezzar then approached the door of the furnace of blazing fire and called: 'Shadrach, Meshach, and Abednego, you servants of the Most High God—come out!' So Shadrach, Meshach, and Abednego came out of the fire" (Daniel 3:26). Because Shadrach, Meshach, and Abednego chose to trust God above the king, the king had a greater respect for them. He knew these were men of character who would not compromise in their commitment to God. In the end the king even promoted them (3:30).

God rewarded the faith of Shadrach, Meshach, and Abednego with His presence. Then He further rewarded them with a promotion. But God also did something else for Shadrach, Meshach, and Abednego they could not do for themselves. He used their faith to point the leader of their kingdom toward the one true God:

> Nebuchadnezzar exclaimed, "Praise to the God of Shadrach, Meshach, and Abednego! He sent His angel and rescued His servants who trusted in Him. They violated the king's command and risked their lives rather than serve or worship any god except their own God. Therefore I issue a decree that anyone of any people, nation, or language who says anything offensive against the God of Shadrach, Meshach, and Abednego

will be torn limb from limb and his house made
a garbage dump. For there is no other god who
is able to deliver like this." (Daniel 3:28–29)

Nebuchadnezzar was an extreme guy, but at least he
got the point. Three men who stood for God showed the
kingdom's top leader that there was someone more powerful than he was—pointing toward God through their
actions and words.

Some people are like that. They will respond favor-
ably toward God only after they experience a person who
stands for his or her faith under high-intensity condi-
tions. Are you ready to set the example?

◩ THINK ABOUT IT ◪

1. Just as a 90-foot golden idol caught the attention
of the Babylonians, there are things today that draw
our attention away from God. What are some of today's
idols? Which of these have the greatest appeal in your
life? What idol do you need to abandon to be more
devoted in your walk with Christ?

2. Paul warned Timothy that those who desired to
live godly lives would be persecuted (2 Timothy 3:12).
What groups in our society today are most opposed to
Christ's principles? What are the consequences of living
a Christ-like life in the world in which you live?

3. Shadrach, Meshach, and Abednego ended up in a
furnace for refusing to compromise their convictions.

What did they experience in the furnace that they had never experienced outside that furnace? How did that experience add value to being thrown into the furnace? What is a difficult situation in which you experienced God's supernatural power in your life?

4. What about you? Are you in the midst of a furnace over refusing to compromise your convictions? Why do you think God is allowing you to go through this problem? What are you learning about Him in the midst of your problems?

5. Who do you know who needs to see you express a radical faith in God in a difficult situation before he or she will be open to God? Are you willing to let God put you through a difficult situation in order to reach that friend or family member?

Chapter 7

412 REVOLUTION

Develop a Lifestyle Worth Following

It was a race like few others in history. As the eight runners lined up at the starting line for the final heat of the event, no one could have guessed the outcome. The group included some of the fastest women on earth. At the end of the day, three of those runners would wear Olympic medals of gold, silver, and bronze. While media consultants had done their homework and figured they knew who was likely to win the medals, this was one time they were completely wrong.

The gun sounded, the runners took off from their starting blocks, and the fans who had gathered cheered wildly for the runners representing their country. For the next four minutes, the focus of the crowd and those watching by television around the world was on eight women running around the Olympic track four times.

The race ended as many had predicted. The strongest runners finished first and were congratulated by their coach and fellow athletes. Nearly seven seconds after the first runner had finished the race, a runner representing a small country that had never won an Olympic medal crossed the finish line. Her coach was there to meet and encourage her. She had finished dead last, but he reminded her there were few who thought she would even make it to the final heat. Back home her friends and family would be proud, even if no one else in the world remembered her name.

But the events of that afternoon would have a profound impact on the results of the race that morning. In an attempt to crush the use of performance-enhancing drugs in Olympic competition, every athlete was tested immediately following the competition. About an hour after the race ended, there was a rumor that the gold medalist had tested positive and would be disqualified. But the real story was not known until much later. *Five* of the eight girls running in that final heat tested positive for drug use. When the medals were awarded that evening, the girl who had finished last became the first athlete from her country ever to win an Olympic medal.

Sometimes the key to winning in life is just staying at it until you finish what you set out to do. The Bible calls this faithfulness.

Faithfulness was important to Jesus. He spoke of it often when He taught. In the parable of the ten servants (Luke 19:11–27), Jesus told of a man who had managed his master's resources well. When that servant gave a report to his master, his master responded, "'Well done, good slave!' he told him. 'Because you have been faithful in a very small matter, have authority over 10 towns'" (Luke 19:17). Faithfulness was the difference. In an earlier parable, Jesus had told His disciples, "Whoever is faithful in very little is also faithful in much, and whoever is unrighteous in very little is also unrighteous in much" (16:10).

Whatever else you may conclude from these parables, one thing is certain. Jesus thought faithfulness was important. It was so important that decisions about rewards in eternity with Him are made on the basis of our faithfulness in little things. You will never realize your full potential as a follower of Christ until you learn the lesson of faithfulness.

Using Faithfulness as a Gauge to Success

When Paul considered the task of equipping a new generation of Christian leaders, he looked at faithfulness as a gauge to measure one's likelihood of success. As we read earlier, he had encouraged that "what you have heard from me in the presence of many witnesses, commit to faithful men who will be able to teach others also" (2 Timothy 2:2). Those who are already faithful in their present task will be faithful when called for greater responsibilities.

That may be why God chose David over Saul. Most countries would not look to a shepherd as a national leader, but God desired faithfulness. David served his father faithfully until he was summoned to Saul's palace to play the harp. Later David returned to his family business just as the nation headed to war. I think David would rather have been at the front, but he set aside his personal desires and ambitions to serve those in authority over him. What David wanted wasn't the most important issue. He served the needs of both his father and his king.

If Jesus is your Lord, you will strive for obedience in the small tasks of life. Peter struggled with this issue at times. While praying at the home of Simon the tanner in Joppa, he saw a vision of a sheet full of unclean animals. There were birds, reptiles, and other animals God had forbidden Jews to eat according to the Law of Moses. But on this occasion, God told Peter to help himself and eat. Three times Peter said, "No, Lord!" (Acts 10:14, 16). Only later did Peter realize that Christ's command was in order to prepare him for an upcoming ministry assignment.

When Jesus is the leader of your life, you forfeit the right to tell Him no. He is only Lord if you obey Him. Paul wrote to Timothy when Timothy was a young church leader among the believers in Ephesus. Timothy was probably around thirty years old at the time.

When he wrote the letter, Paul knew about Timothy's discouragement. The ministry was tough. He encountered enormous problems, including false teaching, believers in his group who struggled with lust, and some who desired to be leaders who shouldn't be leaders.

Writing to Timothy, Paul says, "Physical training is of some value, but godliness has value for all things, holding promise for both the present life and the life to come" (1 Timothy 4:8 NIV). The phrase translated "physical training" is the Greek word *gymnaso* from which we get our word *gym* or *gymnasium*. Exercise is good, but spiritual development is of greatest importance. Why? Because a life committed to serving Christ impacts eternity.

In recent years integrity has become an important word in the corporate world. Increasingly it is also becoming an important concept in business life. What is your integrity *worth*? How much money would it take for you to compromise your integrity? Could it be as little as three cents?

A young man demonstrated all the qualities the company was looking for in executive candidates. It was not long before his name appeared on a short list presented to the company president as a candidate for promotion. The three candidates on that list did not know it, but they had been selected as potential replacements for the president himself. It was part of a long-term transition strategy regarding the president's anticipated retirement in five years.

One morning each of the candidates met with the president and members of the board of directors. While each made a positive impression, one clearly stood out above the other two. Following the meetings they all ate lunch together in the company cafeteria. As the star candidate made his way down the cafeteria line, the company president noticed he placed a package of butter under his roll, hiding it from the view of the cashier who totaled his bill. That action saved him three cents on his lunch bill that day, but it cost him far more than he had bargained for.

When the board met, the young man was clearly the board favorite, but the president vetoed their decision. In explaining his actions, the president told his board what he had witnessed. He had not said anything to the potential candidate, but decided then and there that he was not the man to replace him. "If a man will steal three cents from the company cafeteria, what will he steal from the company when he is in control of everything?" the president asked.

Paul told Timothy, "Don't let anyone look down on you because you are young, but set an example for the believers in speech, in life, in love, in faith and in purity" (1 Timothy 4:12 NIV). Timothy was being discriminated against because he was young. The older believers in Ephesus were using his age against him. The Greek word translated *look down upon* literally means "belittle." Do not let anyone devalue you just because you are young.

That is what Goliath tried to do to David. His purpose was to devalue David as a first step in destroying him. Don't let that happen in your life. Don't let anyone despise you just because of your age. Instead, be an example to those who should be an example to you.

The word *example* in the New Testament means "a model" or "a pattern." This is how to make a difference. The way to silence your critics is to live as an example. Your actions always speak louder than your words. Paul reminded the Corinthians, "You yourselves are our letter, written on our hearts, recognized and read by everyone" (2 Corinthians 3:2). That means we need to follow Christ so closely others will follow Christ if they follow our example. That's why Paul could say, "Be imitators of me, as I also am of Christ" (1 Corinthians 11:1). I love the poem that says:

> You are writing a Gospel, a chapter each day,
> By the deeds that you do and the words that
>   you say.
> People read what you write, distorted or true.
> What is the Gospel according to you?

Are you an example for others of someone passionately following Christ? Be an example, a model, and a pattern to follow. Paul identifies five ways to be an example in the verse we read above from 1 Timothy 4:12.

First, we need to be an example in our **speech**. This has to do with our daily conversations. Sarcasm and vulgar language are not part of God's plan for your life. We are encouraged, "No rotten talk should come from your mouth, but only what is good for the building up of someone in need, in order to give grace to those who hear" (Ephesians 4:29). What does that mean? If it's not helpful, it's not necessary.

This principle is of vital importance. James wrote, "If anyone thinks he is religious, without controlling his tongue but deceiving his heart, his religion is useless" (James 1:26). In other words, the way you talk tells people how important your faith really is. This can even include gossip. Does gossip benefit those who listen? Of course not! Our goal must be to speak words of life that encourage and build up those around us.

Second, God calls us to be an example in **life**. That means our actions. John the Baptist told his followers, "Therefore produce fruit consistent with repentance" (Matthew 3:8). If you are real in your commitment to Christ, it will show by how you live. Your life won't be perfect if you follow Christ, but it will be different.

Third, God calls us to be an example in **love**. Jesus is the ultimate illustration of this kind of selfless love. He gave His very life to offer eternal life to each of us (John 3:16).

Fourth, God also calls us to be an example in **faith**. Do you know what true faith is? When Paul described Abraham's faith, he wrote, "He did not waver in unbelief at God's promise, but was strengthened in his faith and gave glory to God, because he was fully convinced that what He had promised He was also able to perform" (Romans 4:20–21). True faith is depending on God's promises even when they do not always appear to make sense from our perspective. If you are not walking by faith, you can't do all of the other things God has called you to do.

Finally, God calls us to be **pure**. This includes not only sexual purity, but also purity of heart and in our thoughts. You cannot stay pure in your thought life if you continually put garbage in. Garbage in equals garbage out. That's why Paul wrote, "Casting down arguments and every high thing that exalts itself against the knowledge of God, bringing every thought into captivity to the obedience of Christ" (2 Corinthians 10:5 NKJV).

How is that possible? The surest way to be pure is to meditate on God's Word. That is how David did it.

How can a young man keep his way pure? By keeping Your word. I have sought You with all my heart; don't let me wander from Your commands. I have treasured Your word in my heart so that I may not sin against You. (Psalm 119:9–11)

Paul concluded this section stating, "Practice these things; be committed to them, so that your progress may be evident to all. Be conscientious about yourself and your teaching" (1 Timothy 4:15–16). Stay in the Word of God. If you do, these little things will be visible in your life and people will see the difference. They will want to model their lives after your Christianity. You will make an impact for eternity.

Bobby's Story

God calls us to live our lives in such a way that we impact others. If we are not impacting others, something is wrong. One student who made a great impact for God was a boy his fellow students called Bobby. His youth pastor challenged the youth group to carry their Bibles to school everyday. Bobby decided to try it.

After he carried it for a couple of weeks, some of the other young people in the youth ministry complained to their youth pastor. Bobby was not only carrying a Bible to school, he was carrying an oversized family Bible to school. You couldn't miss it.

His youth pastor did not know what to do. He did not want to dampen Bobby's zeal for God, yet he knew there was a better way to be a witness for Christ. But while he was trying to decide what to do, Bobby decided to share Christ with Mike, the captain of the football team.

That day at lunch Bobby walked up to the table where Mike and his buddies and their girlfriends were sitting together. When they saw him, one of the guys at the table said, "Hey, here comes Bobby. Let's get him over here to preach to us." So the boys raised their hands and called, "Hey, Bobby, over here, over here. Come preach to us over here."

When Bobby arrived at the table he said, "I really came over here to talk to Mike."

Mike thought it was a joke so he reared back in his chair and said, "Well, preach to me, Bobby."

Bobby began sharing several verses in Romans to explain the gospel, but when he got to about the third verse, the atmosphere changed. Mike became convicted. He told Bobby he was through listening and to move on. When Bobby tried to read the Bible again anyway, Mike got violent. He knocked the Bible out of Bobby's hand and pushed him back.

Then he grabbed Bobby by the throat, pushed him against the wall, and lifted him off the floor. Even Mike's friends jumped up and tried to rip Mike's hands off the kid's throat. Teachers started coming across the cafeteria as Bobby started choking. By the time Mike's hands were removed, Bobby had slid down the back of the wall, gasping for air as he hit the floor.

How would you respond to that kind of reception? Later that day Bobby met one of Mike's friends waiting for the school bus. Bobby asked Mike's friend if he would like to know how to become a Christian. But Mike's friend was not interested. He had been in the cafeteria earlier that day and told Bobby to move on before he got hurt. When Bobby asked him if he could just read a few verses before the bus arrived, Mike's friend decked him, leaving Bobby with a swollen right eye.

Later that night there was a knock on the door of Mike's friend's house. It was Bobby, complete with swollen eye, holding his big, black, family Bible. Mike's friend thought Bobby had come to tell his parents what he had done, but Bobby had something else in mind. He explained he had not finished reading to him earlier that day and began once again reading from his large Bible.

That night Mike's friend trusted in Christ because Bobby never learned how to quit. Today Mike's friend is a youth leader in his church urging students to carry their Bibles to school every day, even if it means being criticized. Mike's friend knows what God can do through the faithful witness who models God's love as he shares God's message of love.

⊠ THINK ABOUT IT ⊠

1. What does our speech reveal about our inner character? What should be our goal when we speak?

2. How should the actions of someone who follows Christ be different from those of people who do not know Christ? What is an action you really want to change to become a better example as a follower of Christ?

3. How would you define love? How does your description of love compare with Paul's description in 1 Corinthians 13:4–8? As you read those characteristics of love, which ones do you feel you are living out the best? What areas do you want to see improve?

4. What kinds of things cause you to second-guess God? How have you seen God work in your life when you have trusted Him completely?

5. What do you find the most difficult in maintaining an example in sexual purity? What advice can you offer that has helped you during times of temptation in this area?

Chapter 8

WALK ON

Devote Yourself to Christ Regardless of Critics

I t is going to happen. You can count on it. Expect it. As
soon as you decide to get serious in your relationship
with God, someone will tell you that you are crazy.

The student who chooses to live an uncompromising
life in a compromising culture will draw criticism. If you
are not careful, your critics will soon discourage you in
your walk with God and convince you to make the little
compromises that will lead you back into a life of frus-
tration and futility. Don't let it happen!

The late Dr. Jerry Falwell was known for saying, "The
greatness of a man is what it takes to discourage him."
After twenty-five years of serving Christ as my full-time
calling, I have often seen great intentions frustrated
when followers of Christ listen to their critics. Psalm 1

begins with the promise, "How happy is the man who does not follow the advice of the wicked, or take the path of sinners, or join a group of mockers!" However, it is tragic when those who claim to love God do not follow this psalm's advice.

When you decide to set high standards regarding who you will date and how far you will go physically, some people will begin to ridicule you. If you don't continue to stand strong against those who misunderstand your standards, you can find yourself in situations you will later regret. Even if you compromise sexually and don't face a pregnancy situation or a sexually transmitted disease, a condom cannot protect you from a broken heart or broken relationships.

I've also known of a situation in which a student felt God was calling him to attend a Christian university to train as a pastor and was excited to share the news with his parents. However, his parents' first response was, "You can't afford it! Get a job that makes some money."

It sounds so good and seems to make sense, but don't believe it! It's not true! God honors those who honor Him! But the advice of his family and friends does make sense to him, so he puts off going to college for a year and gets a dead-end job. Ten years later he's still at a dead-end job and is not even attending church, much less leading one. Now he's left wondering what might have been if he had listened to God instead of the critics.

A couple of medical students meet at a campus missions fellowship meeting and have a dream of serving God as medical missionaries in a closed country. It is not long before they realize they have a lot more in common and as they finish their training, they get married. They study hard and are noticed by others during their internship, so both are offered work in a prestigious hospital. They accept the work so they can pay down their school loans as they seek God's leading.

When they hear about the work of a Christian clinic in a Middle Eastern country, they just know that's the place for them. But some of their Christian friends are not so sure. "Isn't that kind of dangerous?" they ask. "How are you going to pay for it?" Even their pastor suggests they might want to wait a year or two until the area is safer. They listen to the critics and put serving as missionaries on hold.

Twenty years later he is chief of surgery and she is the best pediatric heart surgeon in the state. They are doing well, and when a missionary from Pakistan talks about a clinic that is underfunded, they write a check large enough to guarantee it will remain open another year. But deep down inside something's missing. They enjoy the lifestyle to which they have grown accustomed, but they can't help wondering how life would be now if they had chosen to make a different decision two decades earlier.

As I wrote this book, I wanted to share the key principles that would help you live for God without compromise. Each chapter plays a vital part in helping you start to live out extreme exploits for God. But starting well is not enough. You must also *finish* well. This is why I saved this material for the final chapter. If you are going to continue well and finish well, you must let God take care of your critics and keep moving forward.

When Friends Become Critics

You will be criticized by different types of people. You will be criticized by those close to you. In some ways, this is the most difficult of criticisms to face. Jesus said, "A man's enemies will be the members of his household" (Matthew 10:36). Job said, "My relatives stop coming by, and my close friends have forgotten me" (Job 19:14).

David found criticism from his family. When he took supplies to his brothers on the battlefield, he asked about *who* would fight Goliath, not *if*. In doing so, David was confronting the army of Israel. God used David to convict them with his simple question. But it was David's brother, Eliab, who became angry and criticized him. "'Why did you come down here?' he asked. 'Who did you leave those few sheep with in the wilderness? I know your arrogance and your evil heart—you came down to see the battle!'" (1 Samuel 17:28). You can almost hear the viciousness in Eliab's voice. He struck right at David's character.

Criticism hurts most from those closest to us. Why? Because the words come from those whose opinions we value most deeply. However, the truth is that the people you love the most are going to criticize you. It may be your dad or mom or your best friend from school. But don't let the hurt stop you. What would have happened if David had turned around and headed home when criticized? Sometimes your moment of greatest influence is just beyond the harmful words of those you care about most.

Criticism also hurts when it questions our motives. Doesn't it bother you when someone questions your heart? It bothers me. The apostle Paul said, "Who are you to criticize another's household slave? Before his own Lord he stands or falls. And stand he will! For the Lord is able to make him stand" (Romans 14:4). David faced criticism for his motives when his brother accused him of pride.

Criticism is also especially painful when it comes from someone you admire and respect. I believe David had two men that he admired. One was King Saul, and the other was his oldest brother Eliab. My daughters love their big brother to death. I think David felt the same way about his big brother. Yet that same big brother was the one who spoke those cruel words: "David, you're nothing. You're irresponsible, you're insignificant and you're immature."

When David heard his brother, he asked, "What have I done now?" (1 Samuel 17:29). That's the way people respond when they feel like they are repeatedly mistreated. David had probably heard his criticism before and he was tired of it.

The truth is that Eliab was the one in the wrong. Not only did he make fun of his brother, but he had also failed to stand up against Goliath. He was the one who was immature because he was the oldest and he should have been the most dynamic, the most spiritual, and the most courageous. When David began to step up in Eliab's place, his brother's anger became unleashed. Eliab started ripping David apart, but all he was doing was exposing what he really was. Your critics may do the same thing.

But I like David's response to his critic. He simply asked a question that struck the heart of the matter:

"Is there not a cause?" (1 Samuel 17:29 KJV). David did not get caught up in arguments with his critics. He kept moving forward to accomplish God's plan for his life. The principle still works today.

Criticism also hurts when it comes from people you are trying to help. David's desire to defeat Goliath would ultimately help Eliab. Plus, David had just arrived with fresh supplies for his brothers. Yet this same brother was now making strong allegations against David.

After fourteen years leading a church, a Christian television program, and a Christian school, I've endured my fair share of criticism. There have been a few very extremely painful moments. What I found most difficult was that those I loved the most and sought to help most were the ones who criticized me most. But David never allowed his critics to stop him, and I've tried to follow his example. David chose not to take it personally. If he had taken things personally, it would have stopped him. He realized that his criticism was not coming from men but from a greater power influencing them—Satan.

When Those You Respect Criticize

David had to face a second critic that day—King Saul. After his episode with Eliab, word soon reached King Saul that someone was ready to challenge Goliath. King Saul summoned this brave warrior only to discover that it was his musician David. When he saw how small David was, Saul was convinced David could not do the job. To make matters worse, Saul took time to tell David he didn't think he could do it.

The people you respect can be the ones who attempt to discourage you. It could be your pastor, youth leader, coach, parent, or teacher. These leaders often provide great inspiration and encouragement. When they discourage you, it can be devastating. When David appeared before his king, he said, "Don't let anyone be discouraged by him; your servant will go and fight this Philistine!" (1 Samuel 17:32).

King Saul was not convinced: "You can't go fight this Philistine. You're just a youth, and he's been a warrior since he was young" (17:33). Saul was living by sight and not by faith. He had it backwards.

When I moved my family to study at Liberty Baptist Theological Seminary, everyone said, "You're crazy!" Why? I didn't have a place to stay, didn't have a job, and didn't have my credits accepted. I just loaded my U-Haul truck, put my car behind it, and led my wife and three-year-old son from our Georgia home to the campus in Virginia. Most people thought I had lost my mind.

I had heard Manly Beasley make a statement: "Faith is believing something is so, when it is not so, because God said so." In my situation, two days after we arrived on campus, we had a place to stay, we both had jobs, and the school accepted every one of my credits. But many people I deeply respected, including some pastors, had said, "Don't go."

When King Saul said, "You can't," David said, "God and I can." Then he went out and did it! David's brother had judged his motives. His king questioned his ability. But Goliath had defied his God, and God's honor was at stake. David knew God honors those who honor Him. He was ready, able, and willing to act on that promise.

I can just imagine that conversation between David and his king: "Let me tell you my story. When I was keeping my father's sheep, a bear came out of the woods to eat my sheep and I killed it. Another day I was keeping the sheep and a lion showed up. I killed him and lived to tell about it."

How could Saul respond to that? God had chosen Saul to lead Israel into battle, but he had failed. Samuel had already told Saul the kingdom would be taken from him. It had been a long time since Saul had seen God working in his life, but he could still recognize God at work in the life of David. All he could say was, "Go, and may the LORD be with you" (17:37).

The Critics We Expect

David's next critic was predictable. His name was Goliath. They were enemies. It was a war. Enough said.

As David looked across to the Philistine champion, his eyes were locked onto the greatest warrior in the region. Taller than an NBA center and equipped with the strongest weapons available in their time, Goliath was physically head and shoulders above his opponent. But David was not overwhelmed by the giant.

Our giants always challenge us and never go away. They keep coming and coming. Like David, you can oppose giants and win if you learn how to battle from God's perspective. You need to build on past victories as you work toward new victories each day. We need success not to celebrate but to elevate. David was not afraid of his giant because he had already killed a bear and a lion in the past. As Paul wrote, "If God is for us, who is against us?" (Romans 8:31).

Get Over It and Get On with It

Those who accomplish extreme exploits don't listen to unspiritual advice. Even great leaders can take your focus from God's true plan for your life. If David had listened to Saul, he would never have defeated Goliath.

You must be bold and courageous to overcome giants and win. David had to convince Saul that he could be victorious. Those who tackle spiritual giants face life with clear purpose. David wanted to kill the giant because that giant had spoken falsely about God. That giant had defied his God. His purpose in life, whether he ate or drank, was to do everything for God's glory (see 1 Corinthians 10:31).

According to Bob Buford, author of *Halftime*, "The real test of a man is not when he plays the role that he wants for himself but when he plays the role destiny has for him."[7] That is what I want. I want to do what *God* wants me to do.

You must be eager to see spiritual victory. In David's case, we are told, "When the Philistine started forward to attack him, David ran quickly to the battle line to meet the Philistine" (1 Samuel 17:48). Goliath had done everything he could to intimidate David. He cursed him and called him names. But it had no effect on David. He was ready for action and in a hurry to win. All he had was a stick, a sling, and a few stones. But as it turned out, that was all he needed. Little is much when God is in it.

Are You Up to the Challenge?

Now let's get personal. I warned you at the start of this book I was looking for a special kind of student—one who was tired of trying to fit into the world and ready to passionately follow Christ. Are you up to the challenge?

Are you up to the challenge of living an uncompromising life in a compromising world? Are you up to the challenge of living Christlike in a post-Christian society? Are you up to the challenge of being 100 percent committed to Jesus? Before you answer, let me remind you what it will take to accomplish that pursuit.

First, you must get off the couch and blaze into battle. The easy option is to compromise and cave into the stresses we face daily. When we come face-to-face with problems, they can overwhelm us. But there is an alternative. It is possible to stand in the power of God's Spirit in the face of your biggest problem and win. Prepare to take on the spiritual giants in your life and win.

Second, you need to settle the authority issue in your life once and for all. James described a double-minded man as "unstable in all his ways" (James 1:8). As long as we waver between opposing worldviews, we will never stand. Daniel found himself living in two worlds, but he made a personal commitment that became his key to success in both worlds. You must do the same.

Next, learn what it takes to confront your spiritual giants and win. A golfer may score a hole in one yet fail to win the tournament. The winner consistently does well throughout the course and does not depend on lucky shots. There are no quick fixes to overcome chronic life issues, but you can discover the key to victory over every spiritual giant you face in life. It is the key that unlocks the door that keeps you from your quest of full devotion to Christ.

In chapter 4 I encouraged you to let God demonstrate what He can do in your life. It may be tough at times and even seem impossible, but that's the point. Only one person has ever successfully lived a perfect life—Jesus Christ. Our key to victory is to let Christ live His life through us, and let God demonstrate what He can do in our lives.

You must take your stand when it is time to be counted. It is one thing to have values. It is something entirely different to live them out. People get in trouble when they begin compromising their core values to fit in better with those who do not share those values. But those who want to become God's kind of person know that when it is time to be counted, it is also time to take their stand for truth. As Ephesians 6:10 shares, "Finally, be strengthened by the Lord and by His vast strength."

Throughout the process you will need to keep trusting God regardless. One of my past students painted the word FROG on one of his car doors. He says it stands for "Fully Relying On God." On the other side of his car, he painted the word PUSH, "Pray Until Something Happens." I love that! Without faith, it is impossible to please God.

The distinguishing mark of the great men and women God has used throughout history has been that confident assurance in Christ's ability to do exactly what He has promised. God calls us to trust regardless of feelings or circumstances.

The kind of person I am looking for will be an example of Christ's love to others. Just as Paul challenged Timothy to be a godly example to others, so you need to be willing to live a godly life before others. That's what it means to live without compromise in a compromising world.

Finally, the kind of commitment I am looking for in Christ-following students today requires moving forward in spite of criticism. Jesus promised that those who followed Him would face opposition. Students who get serious about living for Christ are certain to be criticized by others. Your critics can distract you if you let them, or you can learn from them, let God take care of them, and keep moving forward in your walk with God.

Jesus urged those who wanted to be His disciples to first count the cost. I have tried to explain something of the cost involved in following Jesus. But in all fairness, there is also a cost in *not* following Christ. Several Christians in the New Testament fell into the trap of compromising with the world. When John wrote to the seven churches in Revelation 2 and 3, Jesus commanded five to repent or change how they were acting. To the church in the city of Laodicea He said, "So, because you are lukewarm, and neither hot nor cold, I am going to vomit you out of My mouth" (Revelation 3:16).

There is a cost involved in stepping up to the challenge of living an uncompromising life in a compromising world. Yet there is an even greater cost in *failing* to rise to that challenge. Are you ready to accept the challenge?

⊡ THINK ABOUT IT ⊡

1. Why do we find criticism so painful when it comes from a friend or family member? What are people most critical of in your life? Why do you think people would react in anger to us when we try to help them?

2. Who are the people you respect most in life? How would you discern whether their advice is right or wrong in a particular situation? How difficult would it be to do what you know is right even if they gave you bad advice?

3. Who are the people who are most likely to be critical of your life? How are their values different from your values? Why do you think they are so critical? How do you think God could use these critics to identify real issues in your life?

4. Have you forgiven your critics for their words toward you? Are you holding grudges against your critics, grudges that will turn into a self-destructive root of bitterness? How can you begin to pray more for those who are negative toward you?

5. Are you up to the challenge of living an uncompromising life in a compromising world? As you think through the eight areas emphasized in this book, which do you find easiest to practice? Which do you find the most difficult? Are you prepared to pay the price to be all God intends for your life? What must change for you to be completely committed to following Christ?

THE END IS ONLY THE BEGINNING . . .

We've journeyed through the lives of numerous extreme exploits. Yet the end of our journey is only the beginning of yours. Are you tired of just *living* life? Are you ready to move forward full throttle and ready for action?

Jesus began His radical call to His first followers by simply challenging them to "Follow Me." Leave behind everything you consider important and accept the mission of pursuing extreme exploits in your life beginning now.

Ultimately Jesus left us with two clear commands that encompass all else the Bible teaches. First, we must love God and love people. This is known as the Great Commandment (Matthew 22:37–39). Second, Christ calls us to communicate His revolutionary message of love and hope to all who will listen. Whether at the next desk or cubicle, or to a village on the other side of the planet, our consuming passion must be to share the life-changing message of Jesus in every way possible.

Through a life of extreme exploits, I pray you will change many lives through positive words and actions in your daily lives. To share your stories, please e-mail me at extremeexploits@tntemple.edu. I'd love to hear how God is using you to make a difference.

And if you'd like to connect with others pursuing extreme exploits in their lives or find additional resources, log on to www.extremeexploits.net to join the online discussion and learning. You can also subscribe to the Extreme Exploits e-newsletter or make a request of an Extreme Exploits speaker in your area. May God bless you as you live out your extreme exploits!

Appendix

HOW TO PRAY FOR THOSE WHO DO NOT KNOW CHRIST

The following six principles are those that have helped me the most in praying for God to change the hearts of those who do not know Him. I pray you would use these verses to assist in your own prayers for those who have yet to experience a relationship with Christ.

1. Pray believing.

   "Therefore I tell you, whatever you ask for in prayer, believe that you have received it, and it will be yours."–Mark 11:24 NIV

2. Pray realizing that God is able to do anything.

   "With man this is impossible, but not with God; all things are possible with God."
   –Mark 10:27 NIV

3. Pray asking the Lord to honor Himself by saving the person.

"I will do whatever you ask in my name, so that the Son may bring glory to the Father."
–John 14:13 NIV

4. Pray that the person's eyes, ears, and heart will be opened.

"For this people's heart has become calloused; they hardly hear with their ears, and they have closed their eyes. Otherwise they might see with their eyes, hear with their ears, understand with their hearts and turn, and I would heal them."–Matthew 13:15 NIV

5. Pray against spiritual forces of evil in their life.

"The weapons we fight with are not the weapons of the world. On the contrary, they have divine power to demolish strongholds."–2 Corinthians 10:4 NIV

6. Pray with perseverance.

"Will not God bring about justice for his chosen ones, who cry out to him day and night? Will he keep putting them off?"
–Luke 18:7 NIV

ABOUT THE AUTHORS

Dr. Danny Lovett serves as president of Tennessee Temple University, one of America's fastest-growing Christian colleges. A dynamic communicator, Dr. Lovett has appeared as a speaker before hundreds of thousands of people worldwide. He has authored numerous books and articles, including *Jesus Is Awesome* and *The Good Book on Leadership* (with Elmer Towns and John Borek) and formerly served as the Dean of Liberty Baptist Theological Seminary. Dr. Lovett lives in Chattanooga, Tennessee, with his wife, Susan, and has three grown children.

www.tntemple.edu

Dillon Burroughs is the staff writer for the award-winning TV and radio program *The John Ankerberg Show*, which is broadcast into 185 countries. He is the author or coauthor of numerous books, including the best-selling book *What Can Be Found in LOST?* Dillon is a graduate of

Dallas Seminary and also serves as a professor of youth and culture at Tennessee Temple University. He lives with his wife and three children in Tennessee.

www.readdB.com
www.myspace.com/readdB

ABOUT TENNESSEE TEMPLE UNIVERSITY

Tennessee Temple University is a distinctively Christian liberal arts institution that prepares students for lives of leadership and service.

Tennessee Temple University is characterized by quality academics and biblical values. The university's purpose is to prepare men and women for life through the emphasis on knowledge acquisition, biblical application, skill development, evangelism, and godly living. Tennessee Temple University is multifaceted, with undergraduate programs at the associate and bachelor levels and graduate programs in education, ministry, theology, and leadership. Tennessee Temple University balances a traditional liberal arts program with a historical Baptist position regarding doctrine and conduct. Its unique characteristic is its emphasis on local church ministries through affiliation with the Highland Park Baptist Church of Chattanooga, Tennessee.

Through the traditional residential program and the internet-based Distance Education program, Tennessee Temple University is able to provide a Christ-centered education to a diverse population of national and international students. All classes are taught by dedicated Christian professors who integrate the knowledge of their respective fields with a biblical perspective. The undergraduate university curriculum is built on a foundation of Bible courses for all students, a basic program of general studies, and several major fields of concentration, preparing the student for leadership in ministry, business, education, liberal arts, and sciences, or for graduate studies. The graduate education programs and seminary programs prepare professionals and ministers for service and leadership in their area of calling.

Tennessee Temple University is committed to providing the services and environment necessary to assist its students in achieving their educational goals and enhancing their spiritual, social, and physical development. These include academic support and technical services that assist the students in achieving their goals; administrative services that support students, faculty and staff; and an environment that is conducive to learning.

For more information, log on to www.tntemple.edu or call 1-800-553-4050.

NOTES

1. Robert Young, *Young's Analytical Concordance to the Bible* (Peabody, MA: Hendrickson), 1056.
2. Ibid., 61.
3. Ibid., 259.
4. See Romans 12:21; 1 John 2:13, 4:4, 5:4–5; Revelation 2:7, 11, 26; 3:5, 12, 21; 12:11; 21:7. (All references are KJV.)
5. D. L. Moody, cited by Henrietta Mears, *What the Bible Is All About* (Ventura, CA: Regal Books, 1999), 33.
6. As cited by John Piper in "O Lord, Open a Door for the World," a sermon preached November 12, 1989 and transcribed online at www.soundofgrace.com/piper89/11-12-89.htm.
7. Vaclav Havel, as cited in the inside flap of *Halftime* by Bob Buford as well as in David M. Atkinson, *Leadership by the Book* (Longwood, FL: Xulon Press, 2007), 52.